The Eating Sickness

The Eating Sickness:

Anorexia, Bulimia and the Myth of Suicide by Slimming

JILL WELBOURNE

Clinical Assistant in Psychiatry
Department of Mental Health, University of Bristol

JOAN PURGOLD

Research Associate
Department of Mental Health, University of Bristol

THE HARVESTER PRESS

First published in Great Britain in 1984 by
THE HARVESTER PRESS LIMITED
Publisher: John Spiers
16 Ship Street, Brighton, Sussex

© Jill Welbourne and Joan Purgold, 1984

British Library Cataloguing in Publication Data

Welbourne, Jill
   The eating sickness.
   1.   Anorexia nervosa
   I. Title   II. Purgold, Joan
   616.85'2   RC552.A5
   ISBN 0-7108-0478-4
   ISBN 0-7108-0951-4 Pbk

Typeset in 11 point Plantin by Radial Data Ltd., Bordon, Hampshire
Printed and bound in Great Britain by Butler & Tanner Ltd., Frome,
Somerset

THE HARVESTER PRESS PUBLISHING GROUP
The Harvester Press Publishing Group comprises Harvester Press
Limited (chiefly publishing literature, fiction, philosophy, psychology,
and science and trade books), Harvester Press Microform Publications
Limited (publishing in microform unpublished archives, scarce printed
sources, and indexes to these collections) and Wheatsheaf Books
Limited (a wholly independent company chiefly publishing in
economics, international politics, sociology and related social sciences),
whose books are distributed by The Harvester Press Limited and its
agencies throughout the world.

Contents

Preface

Although much has been written about anorexia nervosa it has proved to be extremely difficult to describe adequately what it really is like to suffer from the illness, either as patient or close relative. The most noteworthy achievement of this book is to have done just this with both sensitivity and understanding.

The authors' approach has a freshness which is untrammelled by exclusive allegiance to one theoretical approach: the excellent results of their therapeutic endeavours amply demonstrate how fruitful a pragmatic attitude can be in such a complex field as this. They eschew jargon yet do not oversimplify. The paramount concern with practical issues throughout the text underlines the fact that the authors' main aim is to care for their patients. Their sensitive detailed awareness of the fears and hopes of both patients and their families demonstrates that they understand a great deal of what anorexia nervosa is about.

Here is accurately described what a day in the life of someone with this illness really can mean. All who want to gain some kind of insight into anorexia nervosa and ways of providing effective help for it should find much of value in this very useful book.

H. G. Morgan
Professor of Mental Health, University of Bristol

Acknowledgements

The authors are grateful to those sufferers who have allowed us to quote from their writings. These extracts are attributed to fictional names but the people who wrote them are real.

The poem 'The Sliding Mountain' from the *Collected Poems of Stevie Smith* (Allen Lane) is quoted by kind permission of Mr James MacGibbon.

Introduction

Anorexia nervosa is the established name for a syndrome which seems to be occurring with greater frequency in Europe and America with every decade that passes. It is a condition which seems to exert a fascinating pull on the imagination of many people both within and without the medical world. In spite of much study there is little general agreement about why people should voluntarily deprive themselves of food until their consequent emaciation endangers their health.

When we decided to write this book, in order to share what we had learnt about anorexia nervosa and associated conditions, there was already a wealth of published material both in scientific journals and in what is commonly termed the popular press. Few, if any, of these articles led to a coherent viewpoint from which it was possible to make sense of all the wide variations of eating behaviour we had seen.

Between the summer of 1980 and the spring of 1982 several new books were published,[1] which contributed substantially to a better understanding of the subject by the general public, but still as late as 1981 it was possible to find in other publications emphatic statements that the cause of anorexia was unknown or inexplicable. Nevertheless the increasing interest apparent in all branches of the media reflects a growing familiarity with the condition among the public. The classically anorexic daughter*

---

*As anorexia nervosa afflicts females far more commonly than males we have used feminine nouns and pronouns when referring to a single sufferer. The sex ratio lies between 20:1 and 15:1.

1

is becoming a stock character in stage and television drama. There have even been anorexic 'jokes' which would probably have been incomprehensible to a general audience twenty years ago (if they had indeed been considered permissible).

In our view it is unfortunate than an idea is gaining ground of the simultaneous existence of a new and different eating disorder called *bulimia nervosa*[2] which has only recently come to light. This new disease is said to be a condition in which the sufferer is a compulsive eater who cannot restrain herself from frantic bouts of stuffing. She shares the anorexic's belief that she is too fat, but unlike the way the classical anorexia nervosa sufferer is viewed, society may agree that the bulimic girl *is* too fat. Her dearest wish is to lose weight. Her family and friends will approve of her attempts to slim and see her goal as a desirable one. The compulsive eater's despair is the result of her non-stop binges: daily repeated proof that she cannot control her eating or herself.

It ought to be made clear at this point that we do not share the belief that anorexia nervosa and the bulimic state are two separate illnesses even though the 1980 American psychiatric classification *(Diagnostic and Statistical Manual – 3rd edition)* makes them mutually exclusive diagnoses. If we need to distinguish and talk about the second state separately we much prefer the description first used by R. L. Palmer. His expression 'the total dietary chaos syndrome'[3] describes the patient's behaviour precisely without attributing any causes to the behaviour. Both those who have been formally diagnosed as having anorexia nervosa and those who have avoided this label can without prejudice be described as sufferers from the dietary chaos syndrome. In our view bingeing is a late development of anorexic behaviour, although the anorexic phase may have been slight enough to escape notice.

We have had classical cases of anorexia nervosa in treatment. Treatment has been discontinued because the family has moved away. Two or three years later they have sought new consultations about 'another problem'. When one hazards the guess that bingeing might be that new problem one may be thought to have telepathic gifts or second sight. But we believe that a girl who gains weight without changing her over-valuation of control, and her erroneous conception that getting thin will be the answer, is not 'cured' of anorexia nervosa. She is simply saved from dying of starvation.

She remains, in effect, an anorexic. While her thinking is still dominated by anorexia, she has one of two options. She can either re-establish the starving state (relapse into classical anorexia) or develop binges. If she tries hard not to binge and *not*-bingeing becomes the chief goal of her daily life then repeated bulimia (nervosa) must follow with consequent weight gain. When she discovers vomiting or purging she can keep her weight steady or let it fluctuate only within a narrow and acceptable range.

The precise derivation of the name *anorexia nervosa* suggests that those who develop this distressing complaint have in fact lost their appetite and therefore do not eat because they find food of any kind to be unattractive or unappealing. (The Greek prefix 'an' signifies being without, and the second part of the word, 'orexia' indicates desire for food. The Oxford English Dictionary defines anorexia as 'want of appetite'.)

The anorexic's relations will remark, 'She never wants to eat anything; there is nothing that appeals to her nowadays.' This is *not* what the sufferers themselves feel.

People who have developed the condition of anorexia nervosa are conscious of having a strong (sometimes an almost over-whelming) interest in food. They feel that their appetite is too powerful. It must at all costs be curbed. The control they exert on their eating is severe. It is only maintained by constant vigilance and the most rigid rules about what may or may not be eaten. The sufferers feel that if their control slipped just once and they ate food not sanctioned by their private rule-book they would 'lose control' or 'go to pieces'. It is their belief that the uncontrolled eating would go on interminably in a fruitless attempt to satisfy their insatiable and demanding appetite. Any letting-up of their iron control would result in weight gain. However thin the sufferer may be she or he will describe the weight gain that could occur as 'getting fat'. This they are utterly determined to avoid. The current view held by most people today is that serious obesity is bad for one's health, fat people are unattractive, and fashionable clothes cannot be found if one is even slightly overweight. These evaluations are pale opinions compared to the revulsion and abhorrence with which a sufferer from anorexia regards the prospect of becoming overweight. For the anorexic *fat* is *bad*. To become fat means becoming lazy, greedy, selfish, sloppy, stupid, unattractive, uncaring, untidy and disgusting. No price is too great to pay to avoid gaining weight. They will undergo any privation rather than 'get fat' and consequently succumb to moral decay.

This preoccupation with weight control and the constant all-pervasive fear of weight gain is the single most important and most characteristic symptom of anorexia nervosa. **If this symptom is not present then the diagnosis of anorexia nervosa should not be made.** No matter how marked the weight loss that has occurred or how long the amenorrhoea has lasted it is not appropriate to call the condition anorexia nervosa unless the girl is preoccupied with controlling her weight. Sufferers from anorexia nervosa spend most of their waking moments (and some of their dreaming ones too) thinking about the food they won't let themselves eat. What makes them different from the rest of us is that they find it worthwhile to deny themselves the food they find so dangerously attractive. 'It's not that I don't get hungry' said a patient to me in the early days of my enquiries. 'It's just that at the end of the day when I've eaten hardly anything all day then the sense of achievement I get makes it all worthwhile. I hate it when I've given in and had something more than the little I had yesterday. I feel I've lost control and I'm miserable as a result. If I've managed on less than I had yesterday – that's great! But that reduced amount sets the new standard which I can't exceed without feeling guilty. If I can manage on that little for one day then I ought to be able to survive on exactly the same small quantity next day. I can *never* increase the amount I allow myself.'

Because what she said has since been echoed countless times by other patients we have to conclude that the term anorexia nervosa is essentially a misdescription of the condition for which it is the established label. Though hallowed by more than a century of usage it can and still does mislead people who take notice of the word's derivation. It would clearly be confusing to try and relabel the condition at this stage of its history. We feel that the fact that anorexia nervosa is actually a misnomer justified us in using the less correct adjective of *anorexic* to describe the patient who thinks in a way which leads to anorexia nervosa while retaining the more correctly derived adjectival form *anorectic* (the version favoured by Professor Crisp and others) for people who have truly *lost their appetite* and feel a marked distaste for food and turn away from the idea of eating. True anorexia is an important symptom of many conditions including sea-sickness, hangovers and many pyrexial conditions such as influenza and hepatitis. It is also one of the common symptoms of severe grief and states of marked depression. Whether we can persuade our colleagues to adopt this distinction between *anorexic* and *anorectic* is at present uncertain. We feel it would be an aid to clarity of thought if our usage were to become generally adopted. For the rest of this book *anorexic* will be used as the chosen term to denote someone who has the central preoccupation with controlling his or her weight and thus avoiding weight gain and 'getting fat' which has been previously described. We leave *anorectic* to the appetiteless.

It should be emphasised that our use of the term *anorexic* is independent of the sufferer's actual weight. It is an adjective which applies to the way a person *thinks*. A patient with anorexia nervosa who conforms to the classic textbook defini- tions of the disease (weight loss of 25 per cent in a young female who has amenorrhoea of more than three months' standing and who indulges in marked food avoidance behaviour) is anorexic in our sense because of her ideas and not because of her emaciation. If her skeletal condition is remedied by a forceful hospital refeeding programme which does not succeed in changing any single one of her cherished values, attitudes and beliefs, she is just as anorexic, in our terms, on the day of her discharge from hospital weighing 8¼ stone (116 lb) as she was on her admission when she was a gaunt 6 stone (84 lb). The way she thinks has not changed. While she goes on thinking on her unchanged anorexic lines she will set about losing the weight she gained at the first opportunity and no ground will have been gained.

In our view *anorexic* is *also* the correct adjective for girls of near normal weight who compulsively overeat and then are so fearful of getting fat they make themselves vomit up the unwanted and harmful food or otherwise empty themselves by taking large amounts of laxatives. *Bulimic* will be used by us to describe the episodic overeating but it is an adjective that we only find useful to apply to patterns of eating behaviour. We cannot find any characteristic bulimic ideas. Peter Slade,[4] a clinical psychologist who has done a lot of work with classical sufferers from anorexia nervosa, describes bulimics as anorexics who do not succeed in restricting their eating. He calls them failed starvers. We cannot delineate any difference in the thinking of straight starvers (classical anorexia nervosa sufferers) failed starvers (formerly thin girls who binge and vomit) or wistful would-be starvers, that is girls whose weight has never dropped much below the average expected weight for their height and age, but who are also helplessly entrapped in the binge–vomit or binge–purge cycle. **The difference between the three groups is in the effectiveness with which they achieve weight loss.** What they are trying to do is essentially the same in each case.

The discussions that occur from time to time in outpatient clinics about whether this or that new patient 'really' has anorexia nervosa seem in most instances to be beside the point. If the girl's thinking is anorexic (that is, if she values thinness as a self-authenticating goal which needs no external justification and she fears to make a mistake of any kind; if she has a detectably low level of self-esteem and she places a very high value on keeping her control of herself and her eating intact) then it is surely irrelevant whether she has 'only' lost 10 lb and is still menstruating or has lost 2 stone 10 lb (38 lb) and has had no periods for six months. In either case she is in trouble and needs help. Can there be any justification for waiting another six or twelve months before further massive weight loss and eventual cessation of mentrual functioning prove to the doctors concerned that it really was anorexia nervosa after all? It is surely not sensible on clinical grounds since research has already demonstrated the effectiveness of early intervention and the danger of delay.

Anyone who has struggled with the difficult and time-consuming task of persuading a dedicated thin anorexic who has a one or two year spell of unchallenged anorexic behaviour behind her that she needs to eat more, let alone that she actually *can* eat more and indeed would be well advised to start eating more *now*, will certainly share our preference for seeing such patients much earlier: *before* they have lost so much weight and *before* they have become so fixed in their ways and set in their ideas. Early diagnosis and prompt referral can avoid some of the more desperate confrontations about eating. Such confrontations should, if possible, be rendered unnecessary, because they are the least fruitful form of contact between therapist and patient. Unfortunately they are still too often essential life-saving measures.

It is still a matter of regret to remember an occasion when a majority decision prevailed against the author's personal convictions. Our hospital team held the view that a university student who was distressed by her frequent bingeing and vomiting could not 'really' have anorexia nervosa because she was not at all underweight at 8 stone (112 lb) and she still menstruated. The fact that she had lost 4 stone (56 lb) in a year (having originally been an obese 12 stone (168 lb) – which was 50 per cent overweight for her 5 ft 2 in height) was not considered relevant to the proposed diagnosis of anorexia nervosa. Those who rejected this diagnosis had not spent long enough talking to the girl to be convinced that her thinking was 100 per cent anorexic. Had they done so, they might have been. She was determined to go on trying to control her eating. She hoped to lose more weight. Her fear was that she would fail to do so. Nothing in the world was more important to her than being thin. Her university was willing to let her take a year off, to recover her health and emotional balance, before she tackled her final year. They were equally willing to allow her to continue her studies without any break. Her university stipulated, however, that if she chose to start without delay she must go on and complete the year. She could not use part of her grant for one term and then ask to fall out for two terms and return later on full grant. She was thus faced with a choice which seemed to her to be a moral one. She was obliged to concede that if her trouble was 'only' uncontrolled eating it *could* not be serious enough to justify taking more time off. Unless she was really ill she ought to continue her course. She had wasted too much time already.

Six months later the hospital nearest to her university had no hesitation in admitting her as a serious case of anorexia nervosa. By that time she had had several months of amenorrhoea and her weight was down to six stone. The graph of weight loss had

continued downhill at an unchanged rate of one stone every
three months: that is, just over one pound each week. She never
completed her degree and she took a long time to get well from
her now undisputed anorexia nervosa. It still seems that our
combined decisions wasted at least six months of her life – quite
unnecessarily.

Diagnostic labels do have some useful features. If there had
been, at the time of that student's dilemma, the current
recognition of the phenomenon now called bulimia nervosa our
colleagues might have been more readily persuaded of the need
to help her at the critical juncture – because they would have
been able to have given her state a sanctioned name.

But despite the positive value to sufferers of this recognition
of the extent and nature of their difficulties we have serious
reservations about trying to set up a totally separate and distinct
category with the diagnostic label 'bulimia nervosa'. These
reservations arise from a failure, as previously mentioned, to
find any recognisable and characteristic patterns of 'bulimic'
thinking. Those patients whose eating behaviour oscillates
between ever more severe extremes of abstinence and gorging
stengthen one's doubts as to the usefulness of making a rigid
separation between these two diagnoses of anorexia nervosa and
bulimia nervosa. On the days when they take nothing but black
coffee the thin ones fit the criteria for anorexia nervosa. Three or
four days later should one change the label for those skinny girls
who have eaten their way through a few loaves of bread, several
packets of biscuits and countless bars of chocolate, only to vomit
the lot down the lavatory? Should one perhaps reserve *bulimia
nervosa* as the appropriate description only for their normal
weight sisters and cousins who have identical cycles of aberrant
eating? Whatever their weight, and whether they are starving or
stuffing themselves, their thinking remains unchanged. Whatever
their eating is like, their over-valuation of control and their
conviction that weight gain is to be feared and avoided at all
costs remain rocklike and undeviating certainties. Compulsive
overeaters think the same way as skinny anorexics think, about
the value of control and the need to avoid weight gain. The
difference lies in what they do.

People act in characteristic ways because of their beliefs,
their values, their unquestioned ground-rules and what they

take for granted. Sometimes they try to act in certain ways but fail to bring it off. It is not clear to us that they earn a separate classification because of this failure. What we have seen is that people who overvalue control, and who experience themselves as failing to achieve what they think they should achieve often resort to controlling their eating and losing weight. The biological consequences of 10 per cent weight loss (approximately 10 lbs for most adolescent girls) makes this control harder and harder to sustain. Some people fail to maintain control of their food intake at a very early stage before their restricted eating has produced noticeable weight loss. Others are good at imposing an iron control on themselves for a long time.

Dedicated intelligent girls who dislike themselves a lot can starve for longer than girls whose previous experience has given them a kindly feeling for some of the physical aspects of themselves. The anorexic's starving of herself must end in one of three ways; by death, a *rare* outcome (approximately 1 per cent in Britain), or by a change of mind – a decision to start eating normally again (a decision which may or may not be hastened by medical or other treatment) or by the anorexic's failure to keep *her own* rules about what she may or may not eat. At this point bulimic behaviour can be said to have begun.

The initial phase of restricted eating and weight loss (or the absence of expected weight gain at the time of a normal growth spurt) may be insufficiently remarkable to get it labelled anorexia nervosa or even weight *loss*. It may be noticed by parents, it may even (in the case of previously obese girls) be welcomed, both by doctors and parents, if the loss is from eleven stone (154 lb) to an appropriate 8½ stone (about 120 lb). But in every case we have seen the bingeing, compulsive-eating state occurs in someone who believes she *ought* to be thinner and who is trying to control and restrict her intake in order to be thin. The binger is distressed because her values, ideas and assumptions are identical with those of the classical anorexic. What is different is that the binger is less efficient at putting her beliefs into practice. She feels she is a failure because she cannot control her behaviour. Like the anorexic she feels it is important to exercise self-control. She grieves when she cannot.

Our experience forces us to conclude that what differentiates ordinary teenage dieting from incipient anorexia nervosa is what the girl thinks, believes and takes for granted as she cuts from her diet all potatoes, bread and pastry and begins to miss school lunch. The future anorexic has no idea of what lies ahead of her if she continues to behave in this way. In other words the eating disorder is constituted by the mental and emotional 'set' which makes control of weight, restriction of eating and fear of getting fat the central focus and predominant theme of every waking moment.

Margery, who, among a lot of other activities, is also doing a little dieting, may weigh the same and have the same rate of weight loss as Violet who is actually beginning an anorexic illness. In this early stage it is their attitudes, values and beliefs (that is, *what* they think about as well as *how* they think about these things) which give such a different significance to each girl's weight loss. Dieting for Margery is simply one of the many things she is doing; for Violet the control of her eating is the central overriding preoccupation which determines whether or not she joins in any other activity. Two years hence, when 9 stone (126 lb) Margery has happily left home to train as a physiotherapist, Violet will be a 6 stone (84 lb) shadow drifting unhappily in and out of hospital. No one, by that time, will have difficulty in seeing the difference between the two. But we maintain it was distinguishable at the beginning to those who were receptive to what they heard, to those who could recognise anorexic ideas and be patient listeners and sympathetic interpreters of faint and (sometimes deliberately) distorted signals. It is in the hope that we can enable more people to make the crucial distinction between Margery and Violet in the first few months of their restricted eating that we are writing this book.

The suggestion by our publishers that such a book could meet a manifest need was reinforced by the comments and enquiries of the many others who telephoned or wrote to us when they heard about our Bristol research project. People made contact with us for a variety of reasons. Some were themselves involved in research or in treating anorexia nervosa. Some offered help and some asked for it, either for themselves or for a relative. We tried to answer them all as fully as possible but there was much we would have liked to add had time and circumstances allowed. We now hope that some of the questions people asked may be discussed more fully here. What we write will be rendered more useful by virtue of the additional experience and insights gained from our two and a half years' work on our research follow up study; the results of which are currently being prepared for publication.

In 1974 Mrs Pat Hartley, then a young research psychologist, took the first steps which led to the foundation of the British self-help group called Anorexic Aid.[5] When she made her interest known in the subject she was almost overwhelmed by the response she received. In her account of that time she said 'many parents and patients described how the initial G.P. reaction often included fear and an open confession that they had no idea how to cope with the illness'. These comments were made in 1974, and they referred to events which had taken place prior to that date, but they are still valid today.

This does not surprise either of us. When in 1972 Professor Morgan asked his newly appointed clinical assistant (and therefore the only other non-rotating doctor in his team beside himself, the consultant) to assume special responsibility for the care of his anorexic patients her reaction was one of equal bewilderment and uncertainty. Jill Welbourne knew nothing about anorexia nervosa at that time and later Joan Purgold similarly had to feel her way in to a useful clinical involvement with anorexic clients and their families. There was no clear guide to the condition. We were encouraged by the Professor's support and enthusiasm and in our early days we diligently followed up appropriate references and read all the available papers in accessible journals. There were few, if any, relevant books at the time apart from unhelpful entries in standard medical textbooks. We were informed but not enlightened. Anyone who has studied the appropriate literature published before 1972 will know why. Not one of these scientific and objective accounts of the disorder explained what we needed to understand if we hoped to communicate with those who had anorexia nervosa. What was the nature of the feelings which pushed people into the anorexic trap and held them in it in spite of its terrible dangers? By what kind of intervention might they be helped to change those feelings so that they could walk, *of their own accord*, out of the trap and into safety?

Since the literature offered no positive answers to these questions we both turned to the nearest alternative source – the anorexic patients – and that was where our real learning began at what might most appropriately be termed the headspring.

Since that time much of value has been published and the former pessimistic view of the illness seems less marked. This is a welcome development. We still believe that anyone who wants to understand what it feels like to have anorexia nervosa can only learn by listening attentively to the sufferers themselves. Much of what is written in the following chapters has been drawn from that source. It is to that first thin, thin, girl ten years ago, the would-be-thinner one we talked to yesterday and to the many more in between that any reader who gleans something from these pages should be duly grateful. They have been our most significant and useful teachers.

NOTES:

1. Professor Arthur Crisp, *Anorexia Nervosa: Let Me Be* (London: Academic Press, 1980; New York: Grune and Stratton, 1980). Sheila MacLeod, *The Art of Starvation* (London: Virago, 1981). Robert L. Palmer, *Anorexia Nervosa: A Guide for Sufferers and their Families* (London: Pelican, 1981).
2. Professor Gerald Russell, 'Bulimia Nervosa: An Ominous Variant of Anorexia Nervosa', *Psychological Medicine*, pp. 9, 429–448, 1979. In this paper Professor Russell acknowledges Doctor Patrick Campbell's suggestion of the term bulimia nervosa.
3. Robert L. Palmer, 'Dietary Chaos Syndrome', *British Journal of Medical Psychology*, 1979, pp. 52, 187–190.
4. P. D. Slade, 'A Short Anorexic Behaviour Scale', *British Journal of Psychiatry*, vol. 122, 1973. In addition to this Peter Slade has published, in conjuction with other researchers, several papers on various aspects of anorexia nervosa. He is currently concerned with the way in which sufferers from anorexia perceive their own bodies.
5. Anorexic Aid, National Headquarters; The Priory Centre, 11 Priory Road, High Wycombe, Bucks.

1 Beginnings

You feel that people will consider you strange, different, peculiar. There are two minds in my mind: the rational, intellectual, detached mind and the irrational, emotional mind: when the body has a need the two minds begin to fight. *Della's self-description. December 1978*

In our introduction we defined the way in which we perceive the eating sickness and the terms we use to explain its varying manifestations, and we acknowledge the sources of our inspiration. In this first chapter we will present the anorexic phenomenon as it has been described by those in whom we have observed it and as we have interpreted our observations.

It is usual, in books like this, to begin with some historical information about the earliest recorded accounts of the illness which is to be discussed together with a note on the origin of the names which have been used to describe it.

Should we copy this practice ? Will it help readers to know that the archives do yield records of extreme fasting behaviour, which sound remarkably like examples of anorexia nervosa,[1] from as long ago as 1500 and even earlier? It is doubtful whether such information can be of immediate value to anyone who, at this very moment, is gravely concerned about the eating behaviour of someone close to them whose well-being seems in doubt. Academic interest is nonetheless legitimate. It may be defended on the realistic grounds that by looking back and attempting to discern the changing pattern of anorexia nervosa and the shifting attitudes of those involved in combating the disease we may learn something which could be of help to us here and now.

Following the description by Simone Porta in 1500 of a fasting girl in Genoa who subsequently died, there were several further accounts of similar fasting behaviour in Europe during the seventeenth and eighteenth centuries. They were few in number. Although written by doctors they seem to express wonderment and awe in the face of behaviour which the writers found incomprehensible. No reliable indication of the incidence of anorexia at that time can be gained from these sporadic reports. There was no medical press and no medical profession as we know them now.

It has been said by at least one commentator[2] that there is no mention of anorexia nervosa in the Bible. Not in the manner of the early Renaissance treatises, it is true, but even the most casual reader will find much talk of fasting in both the Old and New Testaments. The practice of restricting food intake at specified times and for spiritual or metaphysical reasons has existed as long as religion itself. It still exists today as in the faithful observance of the month of Ramadan by devout Muslims. Again we can only speculate whether such ritual fasts ever led into the anorexic trap. There have always been local legends and folk histories of people, usually young women, who developed 'melancholia', forswore all nourishment, 'went into a decline' and died.

No one seems to have considered the question of treatment for the condition until more than half-way through the nineteenth century. Perhaps this is not surprising in view of the numbers of young people who died from a whole range of infectious diseases such as smallpox, pulmonary tuberculosis, typhoid and cholera. These and many more must have demanded the attention of the doctors to the exclusion of the somewhat esoteric eating sickness for which there was still no proper name.

Sir William Gull published a paper in London in 1868 in which he used the name 'apepsia hysterica' to describe the condition of several patients he had seen. Before he reconsidered this name, in the light of further investigation of the biochemistry of voluntary starvation, a French doctor named Lassègue published in 1873 a paper on 'hysterical inanition' in which he referred to 'anorexie hysterique'. The following year Gull independently produced another paper which contains his revised attempt to name the illness. He was the first to call it anorexia nervosa and the name soon became widely accepted (although the French still use the name *anorexie mentale* proposed by Huchard in 1883).

All this and more may be read by those who are interested if they will pursue the references listed at the end of this chapter.[3] Most writers about anorexia nervosa follow the custom of summarising the stages of development of medical recognition of the illness. None, as far as we know, has commented on the fact that 1873 was not only a significant date in the history of anorexia nervosa but also the year in which Elizabeth Garrett Anderson became the first woman ever to be elected to membership of the British Medical Association (BMA). Her comparative maturity at the time of the event (she was thirty-seven) was not due to a late start in her studies nor to any particular difficulty in passing examinations but simply to the fact that it took the members of the Association eight years from the time she qualified as a doctor to accommodate themselves to the fact that although she had become a fellow member of their profession she was not also a member of their sex. Elizabeth Blackwell qualified before Elizabeth Garrett Anderson but the former had gained her degree in America.

The efforts of these women and their successors to enter the practice of medicine were not always wholeheartedly encouraged by the attitudes of their male colleagues. There was even active discouragement from other women, most notably perhaps from Florence Nightingale.[4] Even the encouragement of those who did welcome their debut as doctors sometimes held a hint of patronage.

In case the reader is wondering why we have recalled these particular events let us explain why they seem highly pertinent to us. If the social context in which anorexia nervosa develops is to be considered it must include some observation of the variations in attitudes to sons and daughters and the different expectations parents hold for children of each sex as they enter adolescence. Girls are treated differently from boys but the difference varies with each passing decade. We are forced to notice the effects produced on individual patients by the mores prevailing in the community at any given time. It therefore has become part of our brief to observe closely any local variations in expectations held out to young people of both sexes. We hope in this way to find clues to possible precipitants of the disorder. Similarly the current understanding of these mores by the doctors, nurses and psychologists may affect the basic assumptions of the medical world in which anorexia nervosa is treated. What is taken for granted by her doctor may be crucial to the patient's ability to respond to treatment. When, in the light of those assumptions, instant judgements are made about what her sex life should be without reference to her own beliefs and values, the patient's trust in her doctor is shaken. The intrusion of moral judgements into clinical evaluations can have tragic consequences as Professor H. G. Morgan has described in his paper 'Fasting Girls and our Attitudes to them'.[5] Even now patients are constantly offended by the moral attitudes of staff as when nurses make it clear they think a patient is 'not really trying' to get well.

The history of anorexia nervosa from the 1870s onwards illustrates how it is the attitudes of the clinicians rather than the behaviour and responses of the patients that determine the outcome of events. The illness had found a recognised place in the consulting rooms of Europe and papers had began to appear from countries other than France and England. Everyone had their own angle. The list of papers from Freud reflected the development of his thinking, with 'A Cure by Hypnosis' in 1893 and 'The psychoneurosis of Defence' in 1894, being followed by 'Studies in Hysteria and Loss of Appetite Accompanied by Loss of Libido' in 1895. In 1905 he published three 'Essays of the Theory of Sexuality – Extreme Repression of the Erotic Component in Anorexia Mentale'. In 1914 a paper published in German by Morris Simmonds deflected interest for over twenty years from the psyche to the soma by postulating endocrine dysfunction due to pituitary atrophy. The title of the paper indicates that it was the pituitary gland that was wasted. Somehow the non-German speaking world gained the impression that Simmonds was writing about cachexia of the whole patient due to malfunction in the pituitary gland. When this view was corrected in the 1930s there was still confusion. Anorexics were still sometimes given pituitary extract injections.

The lack of a clear, testable and indisputable physical basis on which to build a formulation allowed the disorder to be all things to all men. We stress *men* because although the illness occurred predominantly in females it had for nearly eighty years been commented on only by men. When eventually Hilde Bruch and Mara Selvini Palazzoli[6] contributed to the literature what they had learned from their experience of treating anorexic patients they were not only read by clinicians but also by some of those who had found it difficult to explain their own eating disorders. In Bristol it was not unusual to see a patient walking into the clinic with a copy of Hilde Bruch's book *The Golden Cage* under her arm. She would offer it as reccommeded reading to anyone who showed a flicker of interest.

Today there is an abundance of writings about anorexia nervosa at least in the developed Western world. Anorexia nervosa remains a disease of what used to be termed the affluent society. It is not much discussed in countries where famine remains a real possibility. In the clinical and scientific journals women are, at least, represented as contributors. The profusion of articles in the so-called popular press, however, are predominantly written by women journalists or by contributors with a personal interest in the subject. The author is often the mother of an anorexic girl, or someone who has recently recovered from anorexia herself, and who is keen to help others to avoid the sufferings she herself had to endure.

With such extensive coverage of the subject it is hard to imagine that anyone has remained completely unfamiliar with the classic preoccupations and activities of the patient in the grip of this distressing and dangerous affliction. Most people have some knowledge of what happens when anorexia nervosa takes over; for many, such knowledge remains vague and unspecific, lurking at the margin of consciousness, until it becomes relevant for them. It may then be incomplete or distorted.

In the interests of clarity let us remind readers of the central preoccupations with control, above all control of food and eating, which dominates the thinking of anyone who has become anorexic. We will quote at greater length from the description of her state written by the girl we have called Della; whose words opened this chapter:

Food assumes a major role in one's life, it dominates all activities. Food and control encircle the self and the self struggles helpless under its command. Knowledge of the self is confused. You do not know if *you* are this strictly imposed control, or if it is dominating *you*. You do not know who you are or what. You act, but you don't know if it is you acting or the control. Both come from within and mingle together in an inseparable fusion. Because you feel so insecure you begin to feel it must radiate outwards – and others will begin to notice it. Your true status and identity are lost; confidence fritters away and one is left alone and naked, vulnerable and cold. One is nothing, one is lower than the lowest.

To those who have, by one path or another, entered the anorexic world this description conveys a clear message: to those who are still outside it may mean little. They are not the words clinicians would use even when they strive to convey the same meanings. In a busy clinic it is probably impractical to take good clinical histories and teach students using the language of poets. Some objectivity is required even in the healing of subjective ills, but we are persuaded by experience that objectivity alone in a healer is no recommendation of his worth and above all not when the patient has anorexia nervosa.

A girl who is thinking and feeling what Della has described will eat less and less and progressive weight loss will follow. If she is persuaded to seek help the diagnosis of anorexia nervosa, tentatively suggested by her family doctor, will be discussed. What has happened to her will be talked about in a language very different from the one Della employed. Although the discussion may include the patient at some point she is unlikely to play a major part in determining whether or not she can be accurately classified as having anorexia nervosa. In all probability she has stated that there is absolutely nothing wrong with her eating habits. Even if she admits to unhappiness or anxieties of any kind she will insist that the unhappiness is caused by her family who constantly harass her over food matters. Her anxiety is the result of worrying about how upset everyone seems to be getting so that she is made to feel guilty about something which is their problem entirely. They could solve it, in her view, by ceasing to preoccupy themselves with her diet. The more articulately she expresses this view the more likely is the diagnosis of anorexia nervosa. If her anxieties about her weight are in reverse ratio to those of the doctors the diagnosis is certain.

In 1972 a set of criteria for diagnosing and classifying the symptoms of anorexia nervosa was established by a group of four workers headed by J. P. Feighner.[7] They were intended to form a basis enabling researchers to standardise their statistical methods. The definition we adopted for research (though it did not limit our clinical work) was based on these criteria:

1 Evidence of weight loss without apparent physical cause (10 per cent of the previous maximum weight or 10 lb to 14 lb whichever is the less).

2 A minimum of three months amenorrhoea (in girls). These two physical symptoms are essential – but the diagnosis is not conclusive without

3 either (a) fear of weight gain which may be directly stated or be implicit in food-related behaviour; or (b) fear of loss of control of weight, again this may be either stated or implied; occurring *together* with (c) concern with control of weight and eating being central and primary in the subject's life: other issues are seen to be secondary to this concern and are resolved only in relation to it.

This constellation may be embellished by a number of additional and variable symptoms but the importance of the last feature, which marks out the subjective dimension, cannot be overstressed. It would be impossible to diagnose anorexia nervosa in a male if that concern with control were absent. It gives the characteristic, predictable and easily recognised rigidity to the outlook and style of the anorexic which is entirely pathognomonic. The additional symptoms which frequently and typically accompany anorexia fall into two main groups:

1 Physical symptoms resulting from extreme emaciation, namely cold blue extremities, bradycardia, lanugo hair, hypotension and so on.

2 Stress reactions which may often be severe enough to constitute a presenting symptom, namely depression, anxiety, obsessionality, or a devotion to exercise which resembles gross hyperactivity.

Feighner's more stringent criteria were designed for researchers; ours were intended as a guideline for our own practice. His would exclude anyone who developed the disease after her twenty-fifth birthday. In the research project in which we were involved, before this book was written, we excluded from our follow-up study those who did not at referral fit our criteria and who never had done so but no one with a problem about eating or weight who came for help was denied it on that account.

What is the description in plain, straightforward, non-clinical language of someone who fits the diagnosis of anorexia nervosa? Let us try to translate the quoted criteria into a recognisable picture of a human being.

Laura is almost eighteen. She is in her final year at school and has a heavy Advanced Level examination programme because she plans to take a science degree and she already has a conditional place at the university of her choice. Before her acceptance can be confirmed she must get grade A passes in at least two subjects and a B grade pass at least in one other. She is, of course, taking four Advanced Levels unlike her class-mates who are studying only the more usual group of three subjects. She has an elaborate and comprehensive work timetable which she devised herself and to which she adheres almost fanatically. This schedule means she has had to give up her activities as form prefect and also as school games captain. The games coach has been understanding and has managed to get Laura's friend to help with the fixture lists and coaching. This girl is no substitute for Laura who was always at the field before everyone else and last to leave after she had made sure all the kit and equipment was in order. Laura is missed in athletics too because she was so disciplined and never missed a training session. Now that she is studying in all the periods when she does not actually have lessons, she keeps fit by jogging after school. She goes at the same time every day rain or shine and always takes the same route so that she will know exactly how much she has done. Her mileage tends to increase slowly; it has never been reduced.

Gradually her friends have stopped calling for her at weekends. She only comes out of her bedroom to go to school, to go running and to get the Sunday dinner while the family are out of the kitchen. She is a good cook and she gets upset if the others don't finish all of the generous portions she puts on their plates.

The family are not worried about Laura's rigorous programme because it was what she wanted. They knew she would want to go to university and get a good science degree because her father had missed his chance. He had had to leave school early and find a job when his father died. He made up for it by his own abilities and has proved to his wife's family that she didn't 'marry beneath her'. You have to put all you've got into achieving the goals you set yourself and, if you do, you'll never fail. That was the family ethos and Laura was not just an ordinary member of the family, she was special as well as clever, everyone said so. She had never failed an exam in her life, or anything else for that matter – as far as anyone knew . . .

When the school games coach called at the house, ostensibly to ask Laura about the summer sports, she asked Mrs Scott, Laura's mother, as tactfully as possible, whether she was concerned about Laura's weight loss. Mrs Scott was surprised at the question at first and assumed it was connected with Laura's training, but the coach explained, with some trepidation, that they'd had a case of anorexia the year before at school and she felt distinctly worried about Laura.

Her mother became worried as well then. She said, that since the children had got older, everyone in the family was so busy with different schedules almost the only meal they had together was Sunday when Laura cooked. Then it was 'I don't feel like it when I've been cooking it all morning, I'll have mine later', or 'No thanks I've been nibbling away while I was getting it.' This was convincing enough to Laura's mother who often felt the same. The rest of the week it was each one for themselves diving into the well-stocked fridge at convenient intervals. No one noticed anyone else too much, except that Laura nagged her father because his regular evening meal had become rather attenuated lately and she accused him of cheating on his diet at lunchtime. He got annoyed when she went too far and rather bossily reminded him what the doctor had said about his weight when he had an insurance check-up and how much he was worrying her mother. He sometimes responded with sarcastic comments about Laura's healthfood fads, her passion for yoghurt and her strict vegetarianism. These episodes were upsetting because disagreements were so unusual in their family. Laura's mother put it down to exam revision in Laura's case. Speaking confidentially to the games coach, Mrs Scott did let slip that her husband *was* under stress at work just now on account of the economic situation. She didn't know the details because he wouldn't talk about it for fear of worrying her.

Laura came in just then and at once her mother felt guilty. She felt wrong because she had been talking about the family and then she saw with a shock what the games coach had seen and which had necessitated this visit. She had in fact been seeing it every day for weeks but till now she had tried to rationalise her fears – Laura would put on a bit of weight once her exams were out of the way. It was good not to carry extra fat, she needed to be lean for her swimming events. Laura knew what she was doing, she was a highly intelligent and exceptional girl and it was not fair to upset her when she worked so hard at everything and was so modest about her achievements. She tried not to upset Laura now by an embarrassed attempt to pretend that changes in sporting fixtures had brought the coach to the house on a games afternoon when everyone else was on the sports field. But the coach was made of sterner stuff. Having surmounted the first hurdle by broaching the subject to Laura's mother, she took another look at Laura's hollow cheeks, at the flesh stretched across her concave temples and at her sunken eyes in their bony sockets and she took the second hurdle full tilt. 'What *is* your weight now Laura?' she asked, brushing aside the social niceties.

There were tears of course. Not from Laura, who was cool, distant, angry, but from her mother who kept apologising for being so silly as to weep. The games coach felt near to tears herself but having got this far she knew she must keep going: there was no way back. She asked about when Laura had last menstruated, a question she knew to be relevant because of what she had seen during her own championship training. Laura's last period had been before Christmas. It was now nearly Easter. Mrs Scott wept again.

It did not end there but what happened, what can happen, what should not happen but too often does, is for another chapter. In this one we are talking about the process of recognising that a problem exists, and identifying what kind of problem it may be. Already the diagnosis of anorexia nervosa seems to be the most probable explanation of Laura's state.

The story of Laura contains enough evidence to meet the Feighner criteria and to include every item on the list of characteristics we find commonly occur in families with an anorexic child. As we have created her we can confirm that Laura does indeed suffer from anorexia nervosa. Statistically her chances of recovery are at this stage very good. Not all those who qualify for the diagnosis of anorexia nervosa have stories as typical as this one. The illness can start by many routes and it does not occur exclusively in young unmarried girls who are about to take significant examinations. Nor are the families we see identical to each other in every respect. They share common themes and present similar concerns and preoccupations in a recognisable manner when they finally reach a therapist but they are all unique. There are no carbon-copy families, nor are patients replicas of one another.

Although most frequently occurring in girls at or around the age of puberty, anorexia can start much later, even in the late thirties. In other cases it can begin at the age of ten or eleven. It does occur in males. The frequency with which it is found in males depends on the interest displayed by the physician. We have found one male with anorexia nervosa for every eighteen female sufferers. Clinics with a special interest increase the proportion to one in ten.

It used to be thought that because the sufferers were predominantly very young girls they would all, therefore, be sexually unawakened as the result of an extended latency period, up to and beyond the age of normal adolescence. Although true of some of our patients this is by no means the general rule. Married people have come with their spouses to seek help. Some new patients are divorced or widowed; others have lived with the latest of several partners for some years; all sought help for anorexia or bulimic difficulties. Both men and women whose sexual orientation is homosexual can be anorexic. In the extreme stages of the illness we have found anyone may become sexually inactive. They will resume their individual love lives once they have recovered. It is even possible to develop anorexia while pregnant – or after the birth of one or several children. Many people, of course, have their children after they have recovered from anorexia as the numbers of patients with mothers who had the disease in their own teenage years can bear witness. Motherhood does not rule out the diagnosis of anorexia. The possibility that the married woman has developed the illness after having one or several children is becoming greater with every year.

We have never heard of anorexia nervosa occurring in the lowest socio-economic groups where no one knows where the next meal is coming from, nor in emergent nations. We have frequently noted the fact that anorexics can be found in families in which there is upward social mobility. We have never seen an anorexic in a family where the change in social class has been a downward move. Neither have we seen one in a family which had no cohesion and no expressed values. In the anorexic's family, high on the list (probably at the top) of the most worthwhile things in life is academic attainment. Not for them the current school of thought which decries the value of the examination system. How then would endeavour be recognised? How would hard work gain its reward? Not for them 'Be good sweet maid and let who will be clever'; their daughter is good and therefore must be clever. All that is needed for happiness is that she realise her potential, and achieve the desired goals.

Once again it is Della's words which explain how it is that a bright, intelligent young adult at the threshold of what would seem to be a life full of splendid possibilities can develop a mode of thinking and feeling which forces her to starve her body while simultaneously demanding from it an ever increasing level of performance. She tells how a closed system has developed, whose working, unchanged by intervention, can proceed logically to ultimate tragedy.

The rational, intellectual mind appreciates that the body has a need, and that this need should be fulfilled. This mind can appreciate that my body needs food, that I need to become fatter, that I need a balanced diet. It accepts the limitations of the body and understands them. The rational will wants the body to eat. The irrational, emotional will prevents the body from having sufficient nutrients; it makes you starve until you can hardly bear it any longer; it tortures the body – forces it to the limits of endurance at every available opportunity. It degrades the body scoffs at its limitations, pushes it on and on. This is most markedly shown in the eating situation but it applies to other areas of life.

One shall not rest when one is tired, until one almost collapses with exhaustion. One must not lie in bed, sleep for a long time. One must work and work. One must not spend money on pampering the body – not buy new clothes, not buy handcreams, not spend for one's personal pleasure. One should live in the meanest conditions possible because one is not entitled to any better – OR one does not NEED any better, any (thing) more. If one receives *more* than the barest minimum one feels guilty – because one is not entitled to it.

Torture begins when the will resists the needs of the body. The needs of the body, represented by the intellectual will, fight against the emotional will. Physical and mental suffering is experienced. Physical suffering can be feelings of starvation, of longing for food, lack of sleep, cold, exhaustion. Mental suffering is the pain of the conflict of wills. Guilt, if one falls subject to the intellectual will, then shame . . . fear.

Fear because breaking out of the control, out of the order means no order. To break out of the strictly-imposed regulations means one has no limits. It means that one will move to the extremes of human indulgence. Guilt exists as flashing images, of reminders of indulgence. It pulls up your spine, creating tension that splits your head with pain, aches in your back and neck, feelings of failure. Barriers of time lock in on you. Clench you in their iron fists. You cannot eat if it is not the right time . . . exactly. Because to break out of this order, again means that control will be lost over the body. If you eat at the wrong time you will turn into an uncontrolled indulger. You may not sleep until it is the right time, you may not stop work until the right time, you may not drink coffee until the right time. Everything must be measured and strict limits are imposed. A certain quantity of a certain type of food is allowed, a certain amount of sleep is allowed. More is not allowed, less is, of course, welcomed. Less is welcomed because through it you exemplify your control. If you could only eat a little less then it is an improvement. A little less, a little less always, is good. A little more is indulgence, lack of control. One must suffer shame, humiliation. Two wills, two minds, and to which mind does the self belong?

The self is battered in the conflict of wills. Is it my self that blindly shouts 'no' to any offer of food that is not yoghurt, banana, apple or muesli? Or is it my self that struggles to assert itself and fails?

We have focused, in this chapter, on the way the medical view of anorexia nervosa developed and on some of the ways it has been described outside the clinical setting. In the next chapter we shall talk about the variations in behaviour someone with an eating sickness may show from the viewpoint of those who, as part of their professional work, undertake the task of helping patients like these to escape from the anorexic trap.

NOTES

1. Simone Porta of Genoa who died in 1554 has been quoted by two Italian authors, Accornero and Baraldi, in a paper published in 1943. Porta was said to have described a fasting girl who died about 1500.

   Pedro Mexio in *The Treasurie of Ancient and Modern Times* Book VI Chapt. 8. (London: Jaggard, 1613) described a French fasting girl named Jane Balan.

   Morton R. *Phthisiologia - or a Treatise of Consumtions* (London: Smith and Walford, 1694)

2. John A. Sours, 'A History of the Anorexia Nervosa Syndrome' in Sours, *Starving to Death in a Sea of Objects* (New York: Jason Aronson, 1980), a comprehensive survey of the subject.

3. W. W. Gull, the address in medicine delivered before the Annual Meeting of the British Medical Association at Oxford, *Lancet*, 1868. '(Apepsia hysterica) anorexia nervosa', *Tr. Clinical Society*, 1874.

   E. Lassègue, 'Hysterical Anorexia', *Archives Generales du Medicine*, 1873.

   C. Huchard first used the term *anorexie mentale*, still current in France, to distinguish the condition from *anorexie gastrique*, 1883.

4. *The Letters of John Stuart Mill* (London: Longmans Green, 1910) contain correspondence with Florence Nightingale on the subject of women doctors and the role of women not only in medicine but in life in general. Extracts from these letters and also other instances in which Miss Nightingale made her views known are recounted in Cecil Woodham-Smith, *Florence Nightingale* (London: Fontana, 1951).

5. Professor H. G. Morgan, 'Fasting Girls and our Attitudes to Them', *British Medical Journal*, 1977, 2, pp. 1652–5.

6. Hilde Bruch, *The Golden Cage: The Enigma of Anorexia Nervosa.* (London: Routledge & Kegan Paul, 1976; Open Books, 1978).

   Mara Selvini Palazzoli, *Self Starvation: From the Intrapsychic to the Transpersonal Approach to Anorexia Nervosa* (London: Chaucer, Human Context Books, 1974; New York: Jason Aronson, 1978).

7. J. P. Feighner, E. Robins, S. B. Guze and R. Munoz, 'Diagnostic criteria for use in psychiatric research' *Archives of General Psychiatry*, 1972.

2 Settling Down to Starving

No one intends to develop anorexia nervosa when they first miss school lunch, or cut bread and potatoes from their diet. The purpose of the initial food-restriction is usually one that the future sufferer's family and friends would unanimously praise. To lose your 'puppy fat' can only make you look better. Everyone knows that dieting takes will power (at least that is the sentence on the cover of the book on slimming produced by *Which?*, the magazine of the British Consumers' Association). Surely no one can complain if will power is demonstrated and self-control exercised? People take it for granted that to be slimmer is to be healthier; so losing weight must be a virtuous and sensible thing to do. Britain's Health Education Council still produces posters which say simply EAT LESS, as though the case for such an instruction needed no argument in its support.

Therefore, when Laura began to lose a few pounds after Christmas we know her purpose was to improve her life and her looks. It is not yet clear why Laura felt that things were going wrong for her at that particular juncture; but readers can safely take it as certain that somehow Laura had become miserable, and felt she was failing at issues that were of the greatest significance to her.

One of our patients wrote this about the circumstances which triggered her initial decision to diet.

Judy moved to Scotland. She was my lifelong friend. When she moved

I was really lost. All the activities we did together I no longer did without her so I was alone. I tried to mix with a new group of school friends. They used to knock-off school and we got into trouble with the police for stealing posters from a shop. My parents were shocked, to say the least, as I had always been quiet and shy and 'as good as gold'.

I was really ashamed of myself but I tried to start again and got myself a boyfriend. It turned out I was too serious for him as he didn't want to be tied down, so soon he started to ignore me completely. This hurt so much I just wanted to die.

At the same time my grandmother died and my parents were preoccupied as a result. Soon afterwards my cat, who was only a year younger than me, became so old and doddery that she had to be put down. This broke my heart even more. I think I was far more upset about her death than about my grandmother's.

My parents were upset and busy with sorting out grandmother's affairs. I couldn't get through to them. My sister had just broken off an engagement so she was unapproachable. My brother was away at university and my little sister was too young to understand how I was feeling. I had no one except Judy, who I wrote to, but it wasn't the same as talking it out with anyone.

For ages I had had thoughts about losing the extra half stone (7 lb) which I knew I would look better without. Mum and my sisters had been teasing me for a long time about my puppy fat. The thing that sparked it off was an article in a magazine about how to lose your 'winter layers'. It gave you a calorie chart and told you how much you could eat each day while still losing weight. I thought I'd give it a try as there seemed to be nothing else to do or to think about as I was so depressed.

What Anna doesn't say, but what is an idea which she and her parents, her brothers and her sisters have always treated as a basic assumption that never needs to be examined or questioned, is that something has gone wrong if you are depressed or sad. They do not see unhappiness as one of the inevitable strands of life which no one can hope to escape. For them it is not a difficulty to be survived; a bad patch to be scrambled through as best one can. They see misery, unhappiness, depression as something that *should not* be there. Its occurrence in their family life means there is a problem to be solved. Something must be done to eliminate the depression. Misery in their family is an affront to their values. It threatens the security of their family life. Unhappiness that will not go away means that feelings have the upper hand; it suggests that control may slip. You might not achieve what you decide you should have. Anxiety lurks unacknowledged because these families are not good at exploring their feelings. They do not let themselves see what is there; they certainly don't talk openly about what disturbs them. But behind the calm fronts the fears increase. Perhaps insurance does not avert catastrophe; perhaps mistakes that cannot ever be remedied do in fact occur.

In a world where death, war, plague and famine are daily realities to be hungry, wounded, ill or unhappy is an accident, the fortunes of war. But in middle-class affluent suburbs these misfortunes are not the standard lot. If it happens someone will be blamed: it feels as though it must be someone's fault.

The sufferer from anorexia nervosa feels this guilt most acutely. 'I ought not to be so unhappy,' wept one client, who had just broken her leg, and who was puzzling the orthopaedic ward by the fact that she hadn't eaten a meal since her admission three days before. But she could not say why she felt she did not have the right to be unhappy. That family rule operated at the level of unexamined, deeply rooted family assumptions.

When this girl was seen with her parents their clear distress at her tearful state gave point to their statements: 'We can't bear her to be like this. We don't understand what has happened.' They loved her and were outraged that she had been hurt in a minor car crash. The fact that her accident was also the means of bringing to light her serious anorexia nervosa seemed to add to their sense of injured betrayal. Those of us working together in the hospital team rapidly felt we were failing to meet their expectations because we could not put their daughter right in a matter of days. They seemed to imply that they had deserved better of us; it was only fair that their intelligent, beautiful daughter should once again be the happy, sweet-natured, helpful girl they were used to having at home. Our failure to achieve this desired result baffled them. After all we were the experts. Her broken bones took longer than they should to knit together and it was a tough prolonged struggle to get Belinda to take enough nourishment to stop losing weight.

The parental bewilderment was not eased by Belinda's determination to hide her unhappiness from her parents because she could not bear to have them worry about her. Our efforts to help Belinda fight free of a deep misery were invisible to Belinda's parents all the while they were protected, by her efforts, from knowing how miserable she really was. They never understood why, even when her fracture had healed, she would not go back to school to complete her Advanced level sixth form course. They hadn't been told enough to let them understand.

Parental reactions will be considered at greater length in Chapter 5. For the moment, let us return to Anna who had decided to lose weight at a time when all her relationships were going sour and she was feeling ashamed and lonely. Did she have difficulty in restricting her food intake? She writes,

Through the summer term it was easy. I always had only a cup of tea at breakfast as I had never eaten first thing in the morning since I'd started school. I went without school lunch and just ate an apple somewhere in the day. Then I'd have an ordinary tea with my family which was the last meal of the day. Weekends were not so easy but I soon fell into the habit of going out for the whole day. I soon reached my target of seven stone (98 lb); I was so pleased and I looked so much healthier, prettier and happier. But the pleasure must have gone to my head for I didn't stop there. *I carried on losing weight.*

By Christmas I was down to 5 stone 4 lb (74 lb). The winter was a nightmare; the classrooms were just too cold to bear. By now my work had gone to pot and I was only thinking about myself all the time. In January and February I was getting worse and worse and the school contacted the children's hospital. I was persuaded to go there for help.

Anna's story is typical. Very few households which eventually produce an anorexic member actually take eating breakfast seriously. People get something for themselves if they have time. Breakfast has usually ceased to be a joint meal years before the anorexia begins. The person who becomes anorexic is often already used to going to midday before she breaks her overnight fast. Her restrictions may at first be fewer and smaller than Anna's were; perhaps she will merely cut out sweets and cakes, bread and potatoes, but will still continue to eat a reduced meal at midday for quite some time. Whether her decline is slow or fast the result is the same.

What nearly all anorexics share is Anna's pleasure at the initial weight loss. They become 'hooked' on the sense of achievement which losing weight gives them. At a time when everything else in their life is messy, confused and going astray here they find a new way of succeeding. Every day the pointer on the scales shows a weight loss; that self-same pointer proves how competent and effective they have now become. This seems to us to be the chief reason why anorexics continue to lose weight after they have reached their original target. To stop losing weight and to stay at a stable (even though reduced) level is to deprive oneself of the sense of achievement; it is to lose the reassurance that the daily step on to the bathroom scales can give. Not that those who have once lost weight abandon their daily weighing even when they try to level off at a weight near their original goal. Then the weighing becomes a repetitive facing of the fear that the weight might have crept up again. If the worst happens and an unintended weight gain occurs the girl will then swing into her old pattern of food restrictions. The overwhelming probability is that she will overdo her efforts. A weight gain of two pounds usually produces a response which causes the girl to lose another seven. This lower weight now becomes the upper limit which must not be exceeded. To lose weight is comforting; weight gain has come to mean failure. She will suffer anything to avoid that outcome.

We have been struck by the significant number of times mothers and daughters have gone on a diet together to lose a predetermined number of pounds, often in preparation for wearing their bikinis on a family holiday. Mother achieves her goal and stops there. Her daughter feels that if losing that much weight was good, losing a little more can only be better. Their original unity of purpose disintegrates and mutual misunderstanding begins. The daughter progresses into anorexia nervosa and her mother is left to wonder in a bewildered way how on earth her daughter's dieting got so out of hand.

In other homes the son or daughter begins to lose weight as a result of a private decision not openly shared with any other family member. The young person then has to cover their tracks and make it look as though his or her intake of food is still what it used to be. Families whose members eat at different times and where each one normally gets his or her own meals for most of the week provide much better opportunities for the young person to get into the anorexic pattern than do families which gather everyone around the dining table for at least two meals every day. In families like these the incipient anorexic finds it essential to acquire a good reason for eating different food from the rest of the family; and preferably a reason that will let her eat at different times from the others.

This need explains the apparent attraction of vegetarianism at this early stage of the illness. An ostensible conversion to vegetarian principles while the non-anorexic members of the family continue to eat meat lets the weight-losing girl make her own special dishes for lunch or supper without attracting a hint of criticism. Indeed she may be given credit for being so helpful and ensuring that her new vegetarian beliefs do not give her mother extra work. Vegetarians are known to eat more salads than the rest of us. A mound of crisp shredded white cabbage and grated carrot can be heaped on a dinner plate and give the illusion that the teenage girl is eating lots of healthy food. She can avoid salad dressings and the hard cheeses like Cheddar and Edam which are rich in calories. She may turn out to be 'allergic' to nuts and unaccountably be averse to soya beans and other pulses. At one stroke her calorie intake is drastically reduced without a single suspicion being raised. After all, everyone has been exposed to countless messages from television, newspaper articles and magazine features which all tell people how healthy it is to eat cottage cheese salads and raw fruit.

It is important not to misunderstand what is being said here. We are trying to describe the 'tactical vegetarianism' which anorexics adopt to camouflage their reduced eating as they slide deeper into the illness. In subsequent therapy it is vital to distinguish these people, who are vegetarians solely for anorexic reasons, from those others whose vegetarianism clearly antedates any eating difficulties and is truly a matter of cherished principle and therefore part of their real selves. It is just as important to support and approve of the abstention from meat of the true vegetarians as it is essential to get the tactical pseudo-vegetarians back to eating the meat they used to like. Being vegetarian because one feels it is morally wrong to raise then kill animals for food does not in itself make it easier to develop anorexia nervosa. An idealistic decision to adopt vegetarian principles does not make subsequent anorexia more probable, though detection may be delayed if the disease does occur.

In the last few years the erosion in value of student grants that has occurred because of inflation has led a lot of students to adopt a lentil and soya bean vegetarian diet simply because it is all they can afford. Against this background 'vegetarian' anorexic students no longer stand out as different. They become unremarkable and can get more severely ill before they are noticed. It may not be coincidence that 1982 saw a higher than usual number of Bristol University students withdrawing from their courses on account of severe emaciation due to advanced anorexia nervosa which had passed undetected in its earlier stages.

What the flatmates of these Bristol students all complained about was the intense interest the anorexic student took in what they themselves ate. 'She'd never come out to eat with us but when we got back to the flat we had to tell her about every mouthful we had eaten. When it was her turn to cook for the flat she got frantic if we looked as though we were not going to eat all she had cooked. She would hardly have anything herself but we had to go on and on till every last mouthful had disappeared or she'd get so tense that life became impossible.'

This complaint recurs again and again in what the families tell us once the anorexia nervosa has been recognised. Mothers report how they have been pushed out of their own kitchens by their anorexic daughters. We hear of brothers who have become seriously overweight through eating everything their anorexic sister has cooked for them. Parents entering their forties or fifties often find their attempts to control the start of their own middle-age spread are blocked by their daughter's insistence that father should finish the last piece of lemon meringue pie and that mother can't possibly go without a cream cake (because then there would be one left over). Parents and husbands have told us that they have habitually eaten more than they wanted to eat at meals so that their skinny daughter or wife would eat something. She would insist on having less than other family members but if they increased their intake hers would go up a little too. 'In order to get her on to survival rations we had to overeat,' said one rueful father.

Our description of what happens to families' feeding habits and eating patterns has slipped imperceptibly from discussing the early stages, when the daughter's gradual weight loss was hidden and unrecognised, to the later stages when her emaciation is so extreme that it is impossible not to notice it and be alarmed by it. This transition is usually similarly unremarked in real life. If a young person is losing a few ounces every day then the change from one day to the next is so slight as to be undetectable. Even the accumulation of lost ounces into a lost pound this week and another lost pound next week can go unnoticed. It seems to take a weight change of six or seven pounds in either direction before the general public can say with any confidence that a friend has lost weight or got fatter.

Anorexics themselves have an almost magical belief that they can see whether they have gained or lost as little as a half pound. Their belief that they have gained weight is rarely confirmed when one puts them on the scales in the clinic. When they are most certain that they must have gained, the scales usually report a weight unchanged since their last clinic attendance. In these circumstances it is a safe bet that something has happened which has lowered their opinion of themselves. They believe they have got fatter because they dislike themselves more – a connection of ideas which will be pursued more fully in a later chapter. In the meantime we hope it is becoming clear why the family who live in the same house as the young man or woman who is every day getting a fraction thinner are the last people to see that the weight loss has reached critical proportions.

Often it is an aunt or other distant relative who visits two or three times a year and who hasn't seen the girl for several months who is so shaken by the amount of weight her niece has lost since they last met that she galvanises the parents into action by her transparently horrified reaction to her niece's appearance. For a moment they can see their daughter through her fresh eyes. They can briefly feel her alarm. A similar response can be produced by school teachers' reactions to a pupil's appearance when she returns to school after losing 10 or 12 lbs over the long summer holidays. If the teachers had seen the girl every day they would have become subtly accustomed to her increasing thinness and it would not have had the same forceful impact. Parents often have a bad press on this issue; and it is usually unfair and undeserved.

People who say, 'How could they ignore how thin their daughter has become?' forget that human perceptions make comparisons and do not perceive absolute levels of measurement.

Most people have some recollections of the experiment in which the subject immerses one of his hands in cold water and the other in hot. After at least a full minute both hands are then transferred to the same bucket of luke warm water. The hand that had previously been in hot water finds the luke warm water cold; the other hand is warmed by the luke warm water. It seems hot to the hand which had been previously chilled in cold water. Yet both hands are experiencing water at the same temperature. In other words what you perceive is determined by your previous experience. The parents find that their child has not changed much since yesterday. The aunt finds that her niece is very different from how she was two months ago. Both are right – but they have had different experiences.

It is the absence of landmarks on the road to anorexia nervosa which makes it so difficult to know when the disease has actually taken hold of the patient or, on looking back, to decide when the illness actually began. Usually the girl will with hindsight give a date for the onset of her illness which precedes by several months the moment when her parents began to notice something was wrong.

Because this discrepancy occurs so often and because it is so difficult to date the onset of eating difficulties with any precision we have come to treat with great caution other workers' accounts of anorexia nervosa which claim that 50 per cent of their cases had amenorrhea as the first symptom, with weight loss coming afterwards.

Certainly a girl who has attained the menarche and then afterwards loses weight will cease to menstruate when she has lost enough weight. The weight loss that is enough to switch off menstruation will vary with the girl's initial weight. Because growing adolescent girls normally get taller as well as getting heavier it is possible for a younger teenager to restrict her eating just enough to fail to gain weight at a time when she is growing an inch or two. Although she has not lost weight she has failed to make a normal weight increase to match her increased height. Her percentage weight (that is, her actual weight expressed as a percentage of the average expected weight for her height and age) has therefore dropped. Menstruation has almost always ceased by the time the percentage weight is below the 75 per cent level. It can disappear when the weight drops into the 80 per cent range.

Provided that an anorexic patient will allow herself to regain lost weight we can be sure that, if she had regular menstrual cycles before she developed anorexia nervosa, she will recover regular menstruation if she lets her weight rise to 90 per cent of average body weight for her age and height and *keeps it there* for the eight to ten months it will take for her endocrine system to get back to normal. In the rare cases when menstruation has taken longer than twelve months to return the sufferer has almost always used the contraceptive pill before or during her illness. Post-pill amenorrhea is not unknown in girls who have never had anorexia nervosa. There seems to be no good theoretical or practical reason why having anorexia nervosa should protect anyone against the development of post-pill amenorrhea. We do not in fact believe that anorexia provides such protection. We do seriously doubt whether amenorrhea ever develops before any weight at all has been lost.

In our Bristol follow-up survey of seventy-eight anorexics we only found two cases where the claim that the illness began with the loss of periods could be plausibly entertained and in both the amenorrhea only preceded the food difficulties by two or three months. The available weight records of the patients concerned were unfortunately not very detailed. The fuller the details we obtained of the circumstances surrounding the start of the illness the more likely we were to find that cutting down on food intake came first closely followed by weight loss. Only then did menstruation stop. Sometimes the initial weight loss was gradual and slight and only known to the girl herself. If the onset of amenorrhea was then followed by a faster rate of weight loss the girl's parents might only report the weight loss that followed the cessation of their daughter's periods. What seems to us more significant about the loss of menstruation is that most girls clearly do not know that losing weight can cause their menstrual periods to disappear. The amenorrhea takes them by surprise and they are usually willing to visit their doctor at this point to find out what has gone wrong.

Some theorists have advanced the view that anorexia nervosa develops because young girls find the demands of emergence into adult womanhood too threatening and disturbing. In their eyes the sufferers deliberately get thin in order to reverse the changes of puberty and switch off their periods and their turbulent emotions by starvation and weight loss.

Our difficulty with this version of a commonly held view stems from the clinical observation than many girls receive with obvious relief the news that they have amenorrhea because of the amount of weight they have lost. It is clearly new information to them that weight loss can have this effect. If it is only getting thin that has switched off their periods then there is no problem because they are quite happy to be their present low weight. 'I was afraid there might have been something really wrong' was one girl's summing-up of her reactions.

It is impossible to believe that if a person does not know that an action A produces a result B she can embark on doing A in order to produce B. If she does not know they are connected she can in no way be thought to intend B to follow her doing of A. Because the doctor constructing his theory does know of the connection he tends to assume that the girls do too.

The fact that 5–10 per cent of all anorexic sufferers are male also makes us doubt the idea that anorexia nervosa is solely a psychological and biological regression to avoid adult woman-hood. (It has never been clear to us to what state the young men are regressing, nor what aspect of womanhood they are avoiding!) Similar difficulties present themselves to us when we consider our married patients who developed their anorexia nervosa when their children were at primary school or while they were pregnant with their second baby.

It might at this point be useful to reassure anyone who may have worries about the effect of anorexia nervosa on female fertility that once menstruation is regained so is the capacity to conceive. Mothers of anorexic daughters sometimes cannot bring themselves to voice their lingering fear that, after all that time without periods when she was so thin and eating so little, perhaps she had done some irreversible damage to her internal organs. After all that, will she ever be normal again, really normal, so that she can have babies? We have successfully treated enough women patients who have then gone on to have healthy babies and raise normal families for us to be sure that the physical effects of starvation are completely wiped-out by successful refeeding and weight restoration. None of our handful of male patients has yet, to our knowledge, become a father so we cannot speak from experience about their state. In our follow-up study there were a number of girls who had had abortions which suggests that the restoration of normal fertility can catch some recovering anorexics unawares.

One of the more sensitive topics in counselling anorexics is that of judging the appropriate moment to talk about future contraceptive methods. For those patients (and there are many) whose anorexia nervosa has produced an accompanying degree of depression it seems unwise for them to risk the side effects of bloating, water retention and increased tendency to depression that some women undoubtedly experience while taking the contraceptive pill. A few pounds of weight gain can be a common result of starting on the Pill. This can shatter the new and fragile confidence of a recovering anorexic who is still trying to learn how to eat normally without risking 'getting fat'. The weight gain is not attributed to the Pill. She feels she must have overeaten though her diet is in fact the same as before she started the Pill. Some unhappy experiences early on have caused us to prefer patients to use non-hormonal methods of birth control. The necessity to become acquainted with the actual ins and outs of their body's construction is an added advantage of learning how to insert a diaphragm correctly. The psychological make-up of an anorexic makes her a very reliable and conscientious user of this method. Other anorexic women have found that the coil or similar intra-uterine contraception device suits their way of life better. It is not, of course, that we suggest that hormonal contraceptives should be forbidden to ex-anorexics; it is simply that, in our experience, the painful and dangerous memories that can be re-awakened by the side effects of most brands of the Pill make their use inadvisable for a surprisingly large number of recovered and recovering anorexics. As reliable non-hormonal methods do exist it seems sensible to prefer them.

We have come a long way from Anna who started to lose weight while missing her best friend, mourning her cat and feeling out of contact with her bereaved parents and jilted sister. It is because Anna's story contained so many elements that frequently crop up in other patients' histories that she has been quoted at such length. The loss of a 'best friend' because the other girl's family has had to move away is perhaps an experience that befalls middle-class girls more often than their working-class contemporaries. If your father and your friend's father work in the local mine then they expect to be down the pit together ten years from now (barring accidents). Men in the ranks of middle-management, teachers, doctors, accountants, lecturers, bank managers, Health Service and local government officers, clergy and countless others in Britain are committed to moving regularly because of the demands of their job or because promotion is achieved more quickly by changing firms or schools. America is an even more mobile society than Britain and in the USA having your father work in the local car factory is no guarantee that he will not go and work elsewhere next year. Nowadays the anxiety seems much more likely to be about whether he will still be in work at all. Losing your closest friend must be a frequent occurrence for American youngsters.

Liam Hudson in his book *Human Beings*[1] reminds us how a close friend can become part of our internal life. We share so much with that friend that his or her departure disturbs both our conscious life and the organisation of our subconscious. Their going leaves a hole and we don't feel ourselves until the wound of their departure heals over. This kind of blow is more damaging to an adolescent who is just beginning to discover his or her true identity than to an adult who already knows himself fairly well, because the loss happens at the time of maximum growth, change and uncertainty.

Similar uprooting and disorienting effects can be produced by having to change schools. Such a move from one school to another cuts off all the developing links with friends and leaves the adolescent without the support of any group of peers. She has to revert to the status of unknown stranger again. It is not always apparent to adults how their children's friendships are ruled by geographical distance. Unless parents allow free use of a bicycle – which in cities is uncommon – the youngster is dependent on expensive buses or the kindness of car-driving older family members to visit anyone who lives out of walking distance. In this age group it is propinquity that makes friendship possible. At sixteen British youngsters may drive a moped or light motor cycle. The independence this acquisition of transport gives can be a transforming factor in children's lives.

Unfortunately the psychological make-up of those loving, concerned, responsible people who are the mothers and fathers of the anorexic patients we see ensures that the parents appreciate only too vividly the dangers of motor-cycle road accidents. While they worry about possible head injuries and consequent brain damage they fail to grasp their children's need to get out and meet their friends without having to plan the meeting days in advance with a bus timetable in one hand and their savings book or money box in the other. Emotional needs are less visible.

When anorexia is taking hold of a young person he or she will choose to walk everywhere. Many parents in fact have difficulty in accepting their anorexic daughter's newly acquired habit of walking or bicycling all over town. They worry whether it is safe for their daughter to be out on the streets alone. As she gets thinner she takes more and more exercise. If she is still, like Anna, eating an almost normal evening meal with the family then she will be unable to sit still and watch television afterwards. If the family possesses a dog it will be taken for some of the longest walks of its life after supper. The walks will settle into a routine because if she goes the same way every time she will know she has covered at least the same number of miles tonight as she walked last night. As her anorexia nervosa becomes more and more firmly established she will probably start exercising in her bedroom and the thumps on the bedroom floor as she whittles her waist and reduces her already skinny thighs will become another constant point in the household's daily timetable.

Hyperactivity increases insidiously. Anorexic daughters and wives probably find it easier to cover their growing inability to sit still than do male sufferers. While the rest of the family is starting to eat their pudding the anorexic female whisks into the kitchen with the dirty plates and cutlery from the first course. By the time the rest of the family are finishing their dessert she has done the washing-up. Over the pile of clean dishes she tells the others not to worry, she had her pudding in the kitchen. Even if they look in the waste bin the pudding will be safely hidden by used tea bags or discarded potato peelings.

In a household whose suspicions are not yet aroused, the anorexic's need for ingenuity in disposing of unwanted food does not reach the extremes of creativity which can be demonstrated in those hospital settings where a refeeding programme is still being resisted by a desperate girl. It may still be enough simply to return unwanted vegetables to the serving dishes and put the extra cereal back in its packet. Certain textbooks designed for medical students make a point of listing the more unusual strategems for disposing of food in great detail. In fact all those people who are willing to shut their eyes and, for a moment, imagine that it is essential not to consume the nourishing drink or food which a nurse has just placed in front of them can usually invent all the commoner ways of disposing of the unwanted nourishment for themselves. If the glass contained deadly poison (which is roughly how a dedicated anorexic regards a glass of milk or Complan) it would be only common sense to pour it down the adjacent wash basin or sink, tip it into an empty hot water bottle or plastic bag, or throw it away out of the window. Pot plants do not have sufficient soil to absorb bulky milk drinks but they can usefully mop up small quantities of glucose syrup, though the plant's flowers can change colour if this is done too regularly. Offering to do the flowers for the ward gives an ambulant girl the opportunity to tip her milky drinks into the vases. Unfortunately, flower arrangements wilt detectably as the milk sours, so this is a short-lived expedient. Most hospitals are reluctant to let a girl go unsupervised to the toilet for fear her food will be flushed down the lavatory, but this route is still successfully used at times.

In psychiatric hospitals there are far greater opportunities. Other patients can be sufficiently confused not to notice if plates are switched and they may end up eating two lunches while the anorexic goes without any food at all. Some psychiatric patients have permanently unsatisfied hungers and will accept extra food from any source. Most mental hospitals have an official policy which bans wards from keeping pets. Nevertheless stray animals are still regularly fed in a few wards. An underfed cat can be a most co-operative partner in disposing of unwanted milk-based drinks, and an intelligent and frightened anorexic will swiftly seize the possibilities offered by such an animal's presence on the ward.

We do not find these actions perverse or strange. If a girl feels herself cornered and trapped she will of course defend herself by any means she can. Devious disposals increase when a frightened girl is coerced into eating more without her fears being understood. The equation *fear plus coercion = deviousness* is almost mathematically precise. If an unconverted anorexic let herself be fattened-up without any moves towards resistance we would be seriously worried at her lack of spirit. The discovery of the strategems designed to sabotage or delay a refeeding programme merely tells the therapist that the patient's fear of weight gain has been underestimated. She has been pushed to make progress at a faster rate than she can bear. It is a warning sign that she has taken covert action to dispose of some food rather than voice her reluctance and fear to the therapist. Before further progress can be expected honest communication must be (re)established. The necessary and useful response is to discuss her fears in a sympathetic and gentle manner, without retreating from the fact that she does need all the nourishment she is being asked to take.

This theme will be developed more fully in the chapter concerned with treatment. It has been mentioned here because we want to avoid even the faintest flavour of reproach when discussing the fanatical moves to which some sufferers are forced to resort in order to avoid ingesting what they see as excessive amounts of nourishment whether the coercion comes from the family or is experienced in hospital.

The dangers of taking a moralistic, judgemental or angry stance on this issue cannot be over emphasised. Time and again the effort to help breaks down on this rock. Fathers are perhaps more inclined than mothers to be explosively irritated when they discover that the carefully thought-out contents of their daughter's school lunch box have been thrown away untasted before she reaches school for week after week. The waste of their money and the fact that their wife's expenditure of time and effort has been rendered useless can make these fathers very angry. They are morally outraged at their daughter's descent into deviousness and dishonesty. The anger is understandable but it does no good. It will probably merely stiffen the daughter's determination to go on limiting her intake of food. If anything does change as a result of father's outburst it will be in the direction of stricter limits and the imposition of more rigid controls. After all, why should anyone change their beliefs and behaviour to please someone who shouts and scolds? Apparently their actions are distrusted and their cherished ideas found to be at fault. Being scolded rarely leads to a change of heart; a bawling-out is seldom the prelude to intellectual conversion.

It is not only food-related behaviour which can try a parent past endurance and lead to an irritated outburst. Anorexics, whose need to stick to a precise timetable is getting daily more urgent and obsessional, can madden parents who do not appreciate their daughter's insistence that supper has to be at 6.30 pm precisely. When the family is visiting friends it seems absurd to turn down their spontaneous and welcome invitation to stay on and eat with them. What does it matter that the meal clearly won't be produced till 7.30 or 8.00 pm? The anorexic will be told not to be so unreasonable; a little delay will not matter just this once. Sometimes it is the degree of her distress about such an apparently trivial and last minute alteration of plan that discloses to previously unaware parents how troubled their child has become.

What action the parents take, and how they respond to the realisation that all is not as it should be with their child, will be the central topic of the next chapter.

NOTES

1. Liam Hudson, *Human Beings: An Introduction to the Psychology of Human Experience* (London: Triad/Paladin, 1978, Chatto, Bodley Head and Jonathan Cape, 1975).

3 The Dilemma of the Family

The terrors of the scenery,
The black rocks of the sliding mountain,
Are hid from the man of family
Who lives beneath the fountain.
His name is Domesticity,
He's married to an ivy tree,
And the little children laugh and scream,
For they do not know what these things mean.
Stevie Smith, The Sliding Mountain

What happens in a family when it becomes apparent that one of its members is starving herself? Initially, at least, it is a private matter involving only the nuclear group around the fasting person. It is no concern of any institution of state, either legal or civil, though at a later stage it well could be. Neighbours, friends, even the extended family are not involved; though often the first intervention comes from one of these either spontaneously or in response to anxious consultation by one or other of those nearest to the subject.

What happens when the person with an eating disorder has no close family ties or is away training or studying and effectively has left home? In these circumstances the family may be unaware of the problem. The whole process of the illness from its unrecognised beginnings to the moment of diagnosis through treatment to recovery may take place elsewhere. The family may know little of what has happened until the final stages. This has occurred a number of times in our experience and doubtless it occurs in other university towns and cities as well. When the eating problem is predominantly of the bulimic or, in the colloquial term, binge-vomiting variety this secrecy is more likely than in the case of straight starving. The starver's state declares itself to any observer. Even if she herself does not tell her parents what is happening others may do so. The binge-vomiter's problems may not be known by anyone except those whom she chooses to tell. We have known husbands to be still unaware of their wife's problem after eight years of marriage.

The families of such detached or independent anorexics, who do eventually become aware that the absent member is in trouble, will be anxiously concerned and may travel long distances to find help, to discuss the advisability of the sick member's returning home or to seek reassurances that help is available. They are unlikely to become deeply involved in the therapy and their anxieties, though often considerable, are not as intense or immediate as those of the families whose anorexic member has not left home.

There is, in addition to the two possibilities of the anorexic being either home-based or away from the parental home, a third possibility seldom if ever mentioned in the literature. This is the patient who is accompanied to the clinic for help by their most 'significant other' outside the nuclear family, usually a boy friend, sometimes a spouse. The extent to which the 'other' becomes further involved in treatment will be a matter for negotiation between the parties concerned but again parents are unlikely to play a major role in such treatment.

Parents whose anorexic child still lives with them are faced in the first place with the realisation that something is wrong with that child. They then try to discover the nature of the problem and their initial feelings of anxiety are increased by their bewilderment at its apparently irrational nature. They not only find the whole anorexic phenomenon incomprehensible, but wonder why such a thing should, like a thunderbolt, strike their family, their child. They may then, in the process of trying to discover how the problem is to be resolved, do any or all of the following things.

They may try to contain the situation, so that outside intervention will not be necessary, by getting the anorexic to resume a more normal diet and gain some weight. Reason and persuasion give way to cajoling and bribes. These are followed by sterner measures. None is effective except in sowing discord and disharmony where, ostensibly, there was none before.

They discover among their circle of friends, relations or hitherto more casual acquaintances someone with experience or first-hand knowledge of anorexia. They may confide their difficulties to this person in the hope of finding a solution within the scope of their own resources.

They turn again to those sources of information mentioned in an earlier chapter – the magazine articles, the press and any of the published material on the subject available to the general reader. They may devise a scheme aimed at resolution of the problem while still confining it within their own domestic boundaries by arranging for the anorexic to stay with an aunt, grandparent or other close contact of family or child. The temporary change of place to live will, it is hoped, be more effective than the efforts of the immediate family in inducing normal eating patterns.

If any of these measures are ever totally successful we cannot, of course, claim to know. By their very nature they are designed to exclude participation by professional advisers whether medical or otherwise. We see only those people whose families have not been able to improve matters by any, or all, of the strategies listed. We learn, when they tell us, what has been tried and with what lack of effect. We cannot know if others have succeeded with these strategies. We only see those who have failed. But we do know, and research has confirmed, that amongst the anorexics who come into our clinics those who recover soonest are those who seek help early.

The process of getting help is often difficult and sometimes more lengthy and frustrating than it need be. It seems important therefore to talk about the ways in which such difficulties may arise.

In our description of Laura and her family in our first chapter we broke off at the point where the first intervention had been made, not by a relative or a close friend of her mother, but by someone who knew and esteemed Laura and who also had some experience of anorexia. This experience, though limited, was enough to persuade her that if left alone Laura's problem would get worse. As this therefore made it essential to get help then obviously the sooner that help was obtained the better.

The history of Laura's decline into anorexia nervosa is not fiction in that every item is true in our experience. Nor is Laura herself entirely a figment of our imagination for, although we have never met a patient of that name (which is why we chose it), her reactions and her ways of expressing herself reflect facets of one or all of those others we have known. Her words could be Della's words; just as her family's feelings reflect what Anna's family felt. How the Scott family deal with these feelings could be the same, in essence, as the ways employed by the families we have known and from whom we learnt what it feels like to have anorexia in the family. Let us take another look at their reactions to the physical education teacher's intervention.

When Laura and her mother were left alone together after their visitor had gone there was a brief interval before the arrival of other members of the Scott family. The unexpected disclosures of the afternoon seemed to have shattered the ordered calm of the household and introduced a note of alarm, fear and guilt.

Neither of them had a well-rehearsed, familiar script to carry them through the time lapse until events resumed their normal recognised pattern. At first the tension was unbearable. Laura's mother tried to break it by apologising for her tears, yet again, with attempted flippancy. To cry had been so unlike her. Laura had agreed and suggested tea. She brought a tray with two cups, China tea with lemon for herself; her mother said she would have lemon as well.

As they sipped it Mrs Scott explained propitiatingly –almost nervously – that she felt it was all her fault. She had been thinking Laura was not eating enough but she knew that her worrying only made Laura feel bad at having caused it. When she'd tried to get her to eat more, Laura either left half the portion or else got into a state of upset out of all proportion to the event. Then everyone got upset which didn't seem fair to any of them. It was not fair to Laura either with the exams only a few months away.

Laura agreed with her mother about not upsetting the others – especially her father who had enough to worry about with the difficulties his company were going though. Mrs Scott was very surprised that he'd told Laura about that as he'd hardly said a word to her. Laura replied that he hadn't but her elder sister Meg, who worked in a large firm of insurance brokers in the town, had suspected it and Meg's fiancé, an electronics engineer, had heard about it through his firm. Mrs Scott was even more surprised that Meg hadn't said anything to her, rather than worry Laura at this particular time, but Laura said no one wanted Mother to be worried and that was why no one had said anything.

All this took the focus of attention away from the original topic of Laura's inadequate diet. When they got back to it the tension had decreased. By the time young Richard arrived from school a formula had been agreed between Laura and her mother which would accommodate both of them. Laura agreed that her work programme was so concentrated that she had literally just been 'forgetting' to eat. She also agreed that her mother could bring her regular trays at the appropriate times so that she need not interrupt her studying. These meals would provide a healthy balanced diet of cottage cheese salads, the occasional egg, yoghurt and fruit. Mrs Scott's collusive response to the suggestion that this was all that was required to allay the fears, anxiety and guilt which had been stirred up by their visitor seemed to cheer Laura immensely. She became quite like her old self, concerned only to spare others from worry on her account. Both agreed her father must be spared. He cared deeply about his children and their academic progress was an important source of interest and satisfaction to him. Their diet, like their clothing and general health, was their mother's concern.

Laura went back to her room in a state of quiet elation. Her mother was an ally. She understood things. She had the right approach and would develop it further under Laura's guidance. They thought the same way. She sat down at the table, drew her note-pad towards her, checked the pages of a physics textbook and glanced at her watch – three hours work to make up. She began writing quickly with one hand as she reached for her pocket calculator with the other. If she could catch up on her schedule before bedtime it would make it all right. The afternoon's visit would have no further significance.

At the school the games coach was talking to the deputy Headmaster who expressed relief that Laura's mother was aware of the problem. With less than two weeks till the Easter break it would have to be left in her hands: Mrs Scott was so capable they had confidence in her ability to take care of the matter.

For the next ten days Laura managed to maintain the status quo in the Scott household. Each evening her mother brought her trays of food which included little 'extras' surreptitiously added to the agreed menu, and cups of coffee made strong to disguise their milkiness. Laura accepted these with a good grace and quietly disposed of the contents in a variety of ways which did not involve her consuming one calorie more than she had done the previous week. No one mentioned weight.

This tenuous equilibrium was threatened by a sense of impending doom. It touched all five of the family, as they came and went about the house, making their encounters with each other edgy and unnaturally polite as they strove not to break the surface tension of the smooth waters covering the dangerous currents below. Twice Mrs Scott tried, with unusual diffidence, to talk to Laura about menstruation. Laura was not sure whether her mother was really more worried about her missed periods than about her reluctance to overeat fatty and unhealthy foods. As her mother was never a gross eater it must, Laura thought, be the periods. She agreed reluctantly that it might be sensible to check this out with their doctor sometime but not till she was through with exam work.

As soon as Mrs Scott realised what was happening to her food trays and milky drinks she made no comment but inferred that Laura had tacitly cancelled their contract. She was thus free to disclose her worries and seek advice elsewhere without further discussion between them. She could not continue to carry all the responsibility alone.

She had decided that she ought to talk to her husband but the next evening, when she was about to do so, she heard the unusual sound of raised and angry voices from the kitchen. Hurrying to investigate she met Laura retreating to her room after a furious exchange with Richard whom she had found taking the last of her yoghurts from the fridge. Mr Scott, entering the kitchen by the garden door, had interrupted by challenging Laura quite angrily on the whole subject of her ridiculous food fads. He was now looking flushed and unhappy while Richard, like the cat who stole the cream, was eating the yoghurt with a mixture of guilt and defiance.

Mrs Scott, always the peacemaker, began to explain in a general way why Laura was justified in being annoyed and why Richard was equally justified in wanting yoghurt. She always believed that everyone had their own good reasons for doing whatever they did and that fusses and upsets were simply the result of not perceiving these reasons. Sometimes it was a great strain on her, being the one in the family who could always do this, and she often wished her husband was more receptive when she tried to explain *why* something happened. Too often his response was 'Well, you should stop it happening again', but he wouldn't discuss how to achieve this end. His own infrequent attempts to alter their children's behaviour were too peremptory for her to emulate them even if they had been effective – which in her view they were not.

On this occasion he seemed ready to talk to her so, leaving Richard, they went into the garden. Mr Scott showed little surprise when his wife told him about the messenger from the school and the anxieties about Laura's extreme weight loss. He said, rather impatiently, that a man at work – the chief accountant – had a daughter who had been anorexic and they had talked about it. Mr Scott had suspected Laura was getting the same way and that was why he'd kept on at her about her ridiculous ideas. She was much too intelligent not to work out for herself that they just didn't make sense. It was probably a phase all girls went through. Boys didn't do it apparently. His tone implied that this was not surprising.

Mrs Scott explained what she had been trying to do to get Laura to eat a little more: she did not tell him how Laura was defeating these efforts in case he made a fuss which would upset everyone in the family as well as Laura. She did tell him how Laura had been sending away all her friends who called to see her, or who rang asking her to go out; even her faithful Matthew who had persisted longer than all the others. Mr Scott was not too worried about this aspect of it, there would be time enough when the exams were out of the way. He did feel that something had better be done about her eating before the examination dates were reached.

Mrs Scott agreed with the need for action. Nearly a month

had passed since the first stirrings of anxiety and four months had gone by since, during the excesses of the Christmas festivities, she and Laura had first considered the advisability of cutting down on the calories.

As neither of the Scotts felt confident of their own abilities to cure the illness, if that was what it was, they discussed how they could obtain the best available treatment as soon as possible. It was assumed that Mrs Scott would be the one to arrange this but her husband told her that she should disregard the cost in money or effort. They could go to London if need be so long as they got one of the top people for this sort of thing; it was too urgent to waste time or take risks. Whatever was the right treatment should be started as soon as possible.

Although Mr Scott had expected his wife to take charge it was he, in fact, who returned from work one day a week later with an address in London given to him by the colleague who had first mentioned anorexia nervosa. It was another three weeks before a series of letters and phone calls had established the fact that it was administratively impossible to obtain the service of this highly reputed consultant. His courteous letter suggested sources of help nearer their home. He mentioned a local psychiatrist who, if he was unable to offer treatment himself, would undoubtedly be willing to give advice as to where it could be obtained.

The very word 'psychiatry' still produces a strong negative reaction in many people in Britain and the Scotts were among them. They rarely thought about the profession and never in relation to themselves. This accounted, in part, for their initial attempt to find help in London. Even though the eminent man they had approached was a member of the dubious fraternity negotiations with him would have had the advantage of anonymity. Distance would have ensured a privacy which their home town might not provide. They had, by this time, not only found out more about anorexia nervosa but had also discovered that it seemed to be more common than they had believed. They were surprised to discover that it had occurred in families they knew. These others had been acquaintances rather than friends but now Mrs Scott was prepared to presume upon the slightest acquaintance in the hope of finding out how Laura's difficulties could be speedily resolved. She talked about her anxieties to anyone she thought might help.

From her researches Mrs Scott learned that some girls who had lost a lot of weight were admitted into general hospital wards where they were under the care of 'ordinary' doctors. There were, apparently, several specialists (physicians not psychiatrists) who were known to be able to produce an increase in weight almost immediately. This information did not come directly from another mother but indirectly from her sister-in-law who used to be a health visitor before she married.

Mrs Scott told her husband at once and his reaction was very much as she had expected. What were they waiting for? What a pity they had not realised about this sooner. Treatment by a specialist physician would not only take care of their feelings about psychiatrists but would also be far more satisfactory in that Laura would get proper physical care and investigations in case anything really was wrong with her. In addition it would be quicker.

It took Mrs Scott another week to fix an appointment with the family doctor and persuade Laura to keep it. She succeeded by letting it be assumed that the purpose was simply to check on the absent periods. Laura would naturally go along to the surgery on her own. Mrs Scott was confident that she would be able to talk to the doctor later; he would probably want this himself once he had seen Laura. She hoped to be able to share her anxiety that Laura was getting thinner; possibly she would be reassured that her fears were due to that famous over-protective-ness so often ascribed to mothers by the authors of many of the articles she had been reading. She was not certain whether Laura was still losing weight or not for, although aware that regular weighing took place, it seemed unwise to risk an upset by asking Laura questions before getting her safely to the doctor.

The summer term was nearly half over and the early holiday season had started for many people including the family doctor. Mrs Scott had been so studiously casual when booking Laura's appointment that her name had automatically gone on to the list of the locum without discussion. Laura decided, when she learnt this from the receptionist, that it was probably better to see a temporary doctor who would just give her a quick check over and then be gone. The last thing she needed right in the middle of the term was a whole lot of visits to the doctor with tests and investigations which might lead to anything.

The locum was quite young and recently qualified. She had done a project on anorexia nevosa in her fifth year and her greatest friend was in the final stages of recovery from it. She seemed to have plenty of time to give to Laura despite a full waiting room. In fact she spent no more than the allotted span for a patient's first visit but she appeared so relaxed and unhurried that Laura was able to explain in detail about her mother's worries over her periods. She also said something about her weight and the worries about that although she had not intended to discuss it.

The doctor even persuaded her to allow her weight to be checked and recorded but she made little comment on the result. She asked Laura if she knew how long she had been the same weight and what was the highest her weight had ever been. She then asked her to come back and see her again in a few days' time. Laura went home feeling slightly puzzled. She couldn't be sure whether this episode would make things better or worse. She *had* managed not to tell the doctor everything – but only just.

After seeing Laura the doctor wrote a referral letter and talked to a psychiatrist asking for an urgent appointment. When she saw her again she told Laura what she had done and explained why. She also said she needed to talk to her parents. Laura felt betrayed. She had, mistakenly, imagined that the doctor's gentle sympathetic approach implied acceptance of Laura's own presentation of the matter. Her parents were persuaded by the doctor to accept the psychiatric rather than medical help by the assurance that two-way consultation between both specialists was quite usual in cases of anorexia. It was explained to them that Laura's physical health would be of importance to both consultants.

By the time that Laura, her mother and by request her father reached the psychiatric clinic the Advanced Level examinations were imminent. The decision confronting those who were responsible at that point was not whether Laura was fit enough to sit the examinations but whether her steady weight loss could be halted and reversed without the necessity of admission to hospital. The decision had to be made in an atmosphere of tension and anxiety. Each of the parties to the decision had a

The Eating Sickness

different notion of what the ideal resolution would be: each was filled with apprehension as to the eventual outcome if their ideas were disregarded by the others.

Laura herself was convinced that events were conspiring to force her to fail. In a desperate attempt to hold out against this consiracy she intensified her work schedules and the ritual observance of her many little rules and strategems relating to her body. If there was to be failure it must not be attributable to her surrender but rather to forces outside her control. She became daily less accessible even to her mother who had earlier provided the main channel of communication between her and an alien world outside a small beleaguered fortress.

Laura's fears were irrational but those of her parents were logical and were shared by the clinical team. They all feared the possibility that treatment would fail unless the initial decision as to the form it should take was a wise one. The parents, in their anxiety, longed to invest all their confidence in the experts. They felt inadequate to deal with the extraordinary problem which, so unaccountably, faced them. Yet simultaneously they were filled with misgivings about the competence of those whose help they sought. They continued to ask themselves and everyone else whether there was not some different and better source of advice, some other form of treatment which did not involve discussing intimate family matters with total strangers.

It was not unreasonable to feel as they did. The possibilities they feared were real. There could be failure. To fail in any sphere of human endeavour is to die a little. The series of negative emotions which it can induce range from disappointment through bitterness to frustration, from rage to final and total despair. The fear of failure can tighten the stomach, drain the blood from the cheeks, haunt the nights, darken the days. We are none of us immune. Often the fear is harder to bear than the failure itself; it can go on longer. Its continued presence can corrode a life to the extent that it becomes unlivable.

The fear of failure experienced by sufferers from anorexia nervosa and by their parents can also be felt by those concerned with the care of anorexic patients. Less personal in its intensity than the family's fear, it can nevertheless produce an acknowledged reluctance to engage in therapeutic intervention in an enterprise whose outcome may be at best uncertain, at worst disastrous. And should therapists be blamed for this? Anyone, whether a parent or friend, psychologist or doctor, who has ever cared for or about an anorexic, will have experienced the sense of powerlessness which is induced in the carer by the condition. To assume responsibility without power is to become totally vulnerable. This will be the situation of anyone accepting the challenge of responsibility for an anorexic patient who is herself determined to defend the anorexic fortress – perhaps literally to the death. We should not blame those who feel unequal to the task and still less those who, having undertaken it, put the physical safety of the patient first. If you undertake to care for someone you are not expected to allow them to die.

Fortunately the possibility of death, though real for a few, is more remote for many of those who come for help although they may be physically unwell and almost certainly unhappy. When the physical impairment is minimal it makes sense to attend first to the unhappiness. Fears about food and eating can only be overcome when the sufferer changes the way she sees herself and develops an optimistic view of her prospects. While the specific fear is still there every meal is medicinal, a part of treatment. She cannot enjoy food until she can enjoy life.

When heroic measures in hospital have not proved necessary the sufferer must do the work herself with the help of the therapist. At such times when , despite regular visits to her therapist, little weight seems to have been gained and her eating habits are still bizarre, families sometimes become discouraged. They lack reassurance and wonder whether they should have done – perhaps even now ought to do – something different. Their despondency communicates itself to the anorexic who in turn reflects, in therapy, the general household gloom. Every domestic event seems to be either highly inconvenient or a downright disaster. The family have become strangers to joy and inevitably the anorexic believes she is responsible; a belief which if not overtly stated is equally not denied. It cannot be denied for there is at least some truth in it.

This is a difficult time for everyone including the therapist. No one is able to take much comfort from the fact that the weight has ceased to fall; although this is a real achievement since it means there has been some change in eating habits. Even the tiny gains measured in ounces are not recognised for the triumphs which they represent. Each one is the result of autonomous action, of a decision freely made by the anorexic herself and worth a pound of flesh produced by tube feeding because there is no secret resolve to shed it again as soon as possible. Nothing has been done *to* the anorexic. She is, slowly and painfully, working her own way out of the anorexic trap.

Treatment seems interminable and unrewarding because the changes are so slow to come. They are slow because they cannot be imposed but must start from inside the anorexic fortress. They must proceed only at the pace which the sufferer can tolerate. To attempt to observe them taking place would be like watching the photographic record of a flower unfolding without speeding up the camera. To be forced to watch such film in slow motion, one frame at a time, is an intolerable exercise but it is exactly how it feels to many families of anorexic sufferers. The families of those who have their anorexic struggle away from the home base will have their anxieties and frustrations but they are spared the daily physical reminders of the slow pace of recovery. They are spared the strain of active participation in a frustrating battle involving constant preoccupation with the commissariat and a marked lack of reliable intelligence on which to base their strategies.

It is this deficit, the lack of intelligence, which many seek to remedy by requesting guidance on the best way to handle the situation. They feel helpless, weary of the whole business. Their child acts as a baffle (in both senses of the word) between them and the therapist muting and distorting communications which, when they do take place, seem relative or incidental rather than purposeful or direct. As the relationship between therapist and patient thrives, their own relationships often seem increasingly fraught with difficulty.

Even their social relationships outside the family are affected. The initial reluctance to discuss the illness may be succeeded by shame and a sense of guilt whenever they are obliged to respond to well-meant enquiries. Their guarded and defensive replies betray rather than conceal their unhappy feelings. Later they take issue with each other about this as they do about everything else to do with the family's problems.

There are effective ways of helping families with an anorexic member and many families have found sources of help, of one sort or another, during the dark days. There is not yet a standard professional method which has been proved beyond doubt and without reservation to be universally applicable and consistently successful. The growing number of health professionals who believe in the efficacy of family therapy sometimes make claims which suggest that it might provide all the answers. Unfortunately the method is not as attractive to all families as it is to these therapists.

Let us not, however, like parents of an anorexic, take issue over the methods of achieving an end which is not itself in dispute. We do want to help families because the anorexic cannot recover alone. Some development must take place which will release them all from their unhappy and dangerous situation. Surely this is what everyone wants? Does there have to be one approach, no choice, no options?

The question, in our case, is academic since we would not have been able to adopt a standard approach to the dilemma of the family even if we had been convinced of the necessity to do so. Such an enterprise requires resources beyond those which were available to us. Even if we had possessed such resources we would not have deployed them in a uniform manner. What Laura's family welcomed may have been intolerable to Della's and, in any case, Della's parents lived three hundred miles away. In every instance, therefore, the decision as to how to help and what sort of help would be most useful and acceptable to the family is an individual one. In the same way that every anorexic shares certain basic, characteristically anorexic ideas with every other anorexic and yet each is a unique individual, so their families share certain ideas and feelings but differ in others. If we do not recognise this we could not communicate with them at all; as we do recognise it we cannot communicate in identical terms with each as though we were unaware of the difference.

This does not mean that we undervalue family therapy or its potential for enabling families to live more happily together than hitherto. It is as attractive to us as it is to most other therapists. We are not, however, totally convinced that all families share this enthusiasm. A family which, for whatever reason, does not enter formal therapy conducted on the model of one of the reputable protagonists, still deserves and wants some help, still needs support and encouragement. Help for the family is help for the anorexic. We have found that the simplest way to decide what form this help should take is to talk about it to the family. What is unacceptable cannot be useful because it will be rejected. On the other hand regular sessions of bland reassurance could be positively damaging by supporting the status quo to the detriment of all concerned. We have, with the co-operation of the family, to work out a compromise between a style so vigorous that it confirms their doubts as to whether they were right to approach us at all, and one so tentative that it merely colludes with the general distaste for confronting negative and unhappy feelings.

By declining to adhere exclusively to one or another of the established therapeutic methods, for which a high degree of success has been claimed, we render ourselves vulnerable to criticism if things turn out unhappily. It used to be common (perhaps it is still) to hear in psychiatric circles a person declaring that they called themselves 'an eclectic'. The description inspired either a sense of reassurance or an impression of inadequacy according to the disposition and viewpoint of the hearer. Whichever view may be accurately held of any particular therapist claiming to be eclectic, all of us are obliged to work out our own theoretical stance without the security of one basic framework to support us. This could be a lonely situation in which to work if there were not so many others sharing it. Most of our eclectic colleagues would, if asked, acknowledge the influence of one or more of the recognised schools or systems of therapy; many would describe their own orientation in terms which seemed to place them in one or other of these schools but would insist that they preferred to work in a flexible way, allowing modification or adaptation, rather than feel committed to a rigid system.

Help for the families who face the dilemma of anorexia nervosa seems likely to be offered in this idiosyncratic way for some time to come. The help that is currently being given varies from place to place and between therapists, counsellors and others. As families also vary, both in their responses and in what they feel is useful and what is not, variations are probably an advantage rather than otherwise. It seems important to us, however, that some fundamental principles, on which the plan for helping will be based, should be adhered to by anyone involved in a counselling or therapeutic role with the families of anorexics. Though we may seem to imply that these underlying principles are specific to the counselling of anorexia nervosa and associated eating problems, in fact, the principles to which we refer also provide the basis of successful counselling for problems which cover a much wider field.

In order to be effective all forms of help need to be freely offered and freely accepted. Imposed help, reluctantly accepted, leaves giver and receiver with feelings of dissatisfaction even if the aims of the helper are achieved. This, of course, is true of all counselling. In anorexia nervosa the position of the family in relation to imposed help is analogous to that of the anorexic patient on whom weight gain is imposed by methods sufficiently rigorous to be experienced by them as an assault on their integrity. Just as the anorexic may then inwardly vow to reverse the apparent progress of events as soon as possible while outwardly appearing to tolerate it, so a family may offer superficial compliance with a genuine desire to achieve the same goals as the helper, but actually tenaciously defend the beliefs and ideas on which their family life depends. Outwardly courteous and deeply concerned for their anorexic member, the family inwardly feels assaulted by the incursion into their private territory of strangers who, like an occupation force, seem to want to change the internal structures on which all the family rely for the conduct of their lives.

Sometimes these feelings are minimal rather than predominant. A family may welcome the opportunity to plan their own part not only in the recovery of their anorexic member but also in the maintenance of progress during the often hazardous phase which follows initial recovery. The fuller their participation in the plan the more satisfactory the outcome is likely to be. The more positive the family feel about their own involvment the less guilt will be felt by the anorexic member. More than one attempt to help families by formal, albeit legitimate, means have in our experience been ineffective because of the additional unhappiness caused in the anorexic by her guilt at being the cause of further trauma for her parents.

We have already mentioned the need which most parents feel for information and the opportunity to talk to the doctor concerned with their daughter's treatment. The satisfaction which this gives can be limited by several things. Contact is likely to be brief and irregular. The therapeutic contract or relationship between doctor and patient would, in general terms, be violated by these enquiries unless the patient gave consent for the information to be given to her parents. In anorexia nervosa, because of its peculiarity or uniqueness, it may seem to those concerned that they are justified in ignoring this principle. If this does happen the anorexic is likely to feel that the therapist cannot be trusted. The message she will receive is that her therapist believes that her parents' wishes and feelings take precedence over her own. She is already sure that this is the case. If the therapist, by what he or she does, confirms her certainty, things will be made harder for both therapist and patient. Little, if anything, would be gained by the parents if such damage were done to the girl.

This compelling reason has convinced us that the anorexic's own individual therapist is not the person who can best help the relatives of the anorexic on a regular basis. The time and attention devoted to regular help for the parents or relatives ought not to be provided by encroaching on the anorexic's own therapy time. Apart from this consideration we have found that it can be more effective if someone other than the patient's own therapist makes it their concern to work with the family towards the successful outcome of the treatment.

Parents and other relatives often find it easier to talk about some of the profound anxieties and painful feelings they are experiencing to someone who is not responsible for the care of their child and who, like them, is excluded from the one-to-one relationship between patient and therapist.

There may be occasions when it helps for everyone involved to meet together. More may be achieved at other times by parents talking, on their own, to someone who can relate to them as individuals in their own right rather than solely as relatives of the identified patient. Even when their child is on the way to recovery the parents of an anorexic still have much to endure. Their uncertainty, anxieties and guilt can become hardly tolerable. Ideally there should be at least one person who will be willing to share their feelings and to help them find a way to change them. They deserve nothing less than this for their own sakes as much as for the sake of their child.

4 Crises of Control and other Complications

The anorexic sufferers who have been featured in our first three chapters have so far all been classical 'straight starvers'. Our three actual patients, Della, Belinda and Anna, were all referred for specialist help while their weight was still declining and they remained dedicated to managing on less food with every day that passed. The unfolding saga of the invented Scott family contains no hint that Laura has yet had trouble in maintaining her iron control. The weight graphs of all four show a relentless decline. And yet it is clear that by no means all of those whose thinking becomes anorexic continue to lose weight steadily to the point of physical collapse. As we briefly indicated in our introduction, there can come a point where a sufferer breaks her own rules and hastily starts to cram into her mouth some forbidden sweet stuff or other fattening foods.

The moment when control snaps comes very late for some sufferers and very early for others. We are still struggling to catalogue the factors which produce this breakdown of the highly valued and formerly rigid control. Some of those which recur in the stories told to us are factors which are well known to lead to rule-breaking behaviour in other fields. Having too much to drink can lead habitually chaste girls to lose their inhibitions at a party and end up in bed with a man. Too much alcohol can also be the prelude to a former starver uncharacteristically demolishing an untouched loaf of bread and half a pound of butter. It is often the anorexic who has 'fallen' for the sinful fats and carbohydrates who feels more guilty and humiliated when she realises what she has done. By comparison with the horror she feels at her failure of will-power, the unintended loss of virginity could seem a minor matter for regret.

It is not merely excess alcohol which can provide the trigger for the first bout of compulsive eating. Binges can also occur when the formerly starving girl is exhausted by lack of sleep or has had an emotional shock or rare burst of crying. Some unfortunates have actually experienced their first binges while sleep-walking; for others the state of just waking up but not yet reaching full alertness has been the moment when their food-control first slipped.

What is critical at this point is not what triggered the first bout of over-eating but what is the sufferer's response to its occurrence. It is difficult for established bingers to believe that their efforts to re-establish the slipping control are the very thing which causes their control to go to pieces. Characteristically anorexics respond to the first shocking binge by trying to re-establish an even more strict control of their food intake than they had before. 'If at first you don't succeed then try, try again', is the precept that their upbringing has instilled into them as the chief way to solve problems. Without pausing, even for a moment, to consider the wisdom of what they are trying to do the universal response of those anorexics who have binged for the first time is to redouble their efforts to exercise control. If they were allowing themselves a boiled egg for lunch before the binge then afterwards they will eat only the yolk and throw away the white. More of the same is their solution. It has not occurred to a single sufferer to stop and wonder whether it might be better to do something different instead. They do not question the necessity for control; they merely strive to exercise greater control more often.

In this attitude lies the seeds of the next failure. Anything a human being accomplishes by the exercise of will-power alone, against the pull of natural inclinations, will not be sustained for long. A man cannot go on being charming to the irritating mother-in-law whose visits he resents if he relies solely on will-power. Sooner or later the facade of charm will crack and he will vent his irritation. The explosion will be the greater the longer the irritation has been held in check by sheer will-power.

In just the same way the first binge will be followed by a second. We are now certain that the length and ferocity of the subsequent binges are directly proportional to the severity and duration of the preceding periods of fasting. The oscillation between having and not-having, between starving and stuffing, gets more and more violent. Patients have eventually developed patterns where they live for a week or more on nothing but black coffee and then empty the parental larder overnight in a twelve hour marathon of non-stop eating. They then return to the black coffee diet feeling guilty and disgusting.

When bingeing starts the foodstuffs that are eaten are the ones the girl finds attractive but fears will be fattening. For an established binger, who has yet again fallen victim to the compulsion to eat and eat, any kind of food will do. When food stocks are low desperate beings will rescue discarded bread crusts or mouldy cheese from the waste bin. Biscuits and chocolate can be taken from other students' lockers without a thought for the eventual reactions of the original owners. The milk for tomorrow's breakfast, the iced cake ready for a fellow student's birthday celebration, the trifle awaiting the parents' dinner guests; all have been devoured regardless of later consequences when the craving to eat overcame the failed starver yet once again.

In the extreme versions of these compulsive bouts of overeating the calories consumed in a couple of hours can total three or four times as much as a normal adult would eat in a whole day. It is of course impossible to overeat repeatedly on this scale without rapid and massive weight gain.

The distress that follows bingeing and subsequent weight gain is overwhelming. The guilt and misery confines the remorseful binger to his or her room. Any excuse is made that will cover the failure to arrive at work or college because it is of course impossible to let yourself be seen until the effects of the binge have been undone. The anorexic who has started to binge will at first show a see-saw in his or her weight chart. With time the peaks and troughs are sharper. Each rise in the weight graph is paralleled by an emotional plunge into despair. The immediate post-binge phase is the moment above all others when the anorexic who can no longer pride herself on the control she used to exert and the weight loss she formerly achieved feels that life is not worth living.

In a moment when nothing exists for her but disgust with herself and horrified revulsion from what she has done she may make an impulsive but determined attempt to kill herself. It is only when sufferers have already made a relationship with an understanding friend or counsellor that it is possible to relieve the distress by making an emergency 'phone call instead. It is impossible to seek help *for the first time* in the turmoil of a binge or during its aftermath.

At first binges may be twice-weekly events, later once a day or more. No human being can bear the extremes of humiliation, fear, despair and disgust which bingers experience without seeking ways to soften the consequences of what they have done. It is bad enough to have eaten all that 'junk' food without having to get fat overnight as well. The idea that vomiting would relieve both the distended stomach and the overburdened spirit may be 'invented' by the sufferer or may be suggested to her by something she reads or someone she meets. At first it is necessary to induce vomiting by drinking salt and water or by sticking a finger or two down your own throat. Doing this over and over again day after day can cause ulcers or callouses on the hand where the top row of front teeth catches the skin of the hand just around the knuckle of the index finger. Repetition makes it easier and easier to be sick. Practised vomiters have merely to stand by the lavatory and tense their stomach muscles to throw up with ease. After a while vomiting becomes a conditioned response which automatically follows once a certain degree of abdominal distension or stomach filling has been attained. Once this stage has been reached even meals which people do want to keep down cannot be retained without a struggle that can bring sweat to the sufferer's forehead.

It is not everyone who can vomit. The ability to make yourself sick varies between one individual and another. Those unfortunates who cannot ever make themselves vomit have to turn to the only other means by which the unwanted junk food they have consumed can be removed from their bodies before it makes them fat. What cannot be thrown up must be forced through and rushed out of the digestive tract's only other aperture. The use of laxatives to purge oneself of unwanted food again can be an independent invention or it can be a technique first explored because of some other person's suggestion.

There is an inevitable escalation here too. The bowel becomes tolerant of the initial dose of purgatives and no longer responds. The sufferer doubles the dose and is relieved when once more the technique works and she or he spends most of next day on the lavatory. But sooner or later the dose will have to be increased again. Years of undetected purging can so build up tolerance for certain laxatives that patients have been seen who were taking 50–70 Senokot tablets each day. This regular consumption of more than thirty times the recommended daily dose has damaging long-term effects on the bowel. As Victorian physicians knew only too well this amount of purgatives can lead to selective poisoning of some of the nerve endings supplying the muscle fibres in the coats of the intestine. The resultant non-functioning of parts of the conductive network means that peristalsis is rendered inefficient and the bowel can no longer produce smoothly co-ordinated waves of contraction.

Achieving a daily bowel action becomes more and more difficult. One of our more unexpected clinical findings was that patients who have regularly used larger-than-normal quantities of laxatives develop a characteristic distension of their upper digestive tract after eating anything like a normal-size meal. 'It's suddenly just as though she's got a hollow melon in her tummy' was one husband's description of his wife's state after a rare evening out. The patient complains of bloating, distension and abdominal discomfort. This latter can sometimes be severe enough to amount to acute cramps. The pain can make it impossible to carry on with any ordinary household activity, though this would be an unusually severe response. This particular pattern of distension, which comes on sharply after the ingestion of food *and which is clearly visible to an observer* and can be felt by an examiner's hand, has several times been the sole cause of our correctly supposing the patient to be in deep trouble over laxative use. It is important not to suspect excessive laxative consumption simply because the patient *complains* of bloating. Many anorexics suffer discomfort from what other people seem to accept as normal abdominal gurglings. The clue lies in the intermittently palpable and gas-distended upper abdomen.

Patients who have developed this complication can be

reassured that, if they reduce their intake of laxatives step by step until they finally cease to take any at all, they will find the abdominal distension after eating gradually diminishes also until it ceases to be a problem. There can be a lag in that the distension may not improve as soon as fewer tablets start to be taken; but everyone under thirty-five who has cut down and finally stopped using purgatives has found that distension problems become increasingly insignificant as time goes by. Our experience with older patients is too small for us to draw any certain conclusions. We do get an impression that the older the person is the longer the digestive tract may take before it returns to normal. Step by step reduction of the amounts of laxative tablets taken each day is advised because the bowel seems to cease its waste disposal function with uncomfortable suddenness if the sufferer just stops using laxatives overnight. There are few more distressing physical states than the collapse produced by a colicky crisis of total constipation, and the resolution of such a crisis requires uncomfortable and undignified measures.

The other physical hazard faced both by purgers and vomiters is that of upsetting the biochemical balance of the body. When excess food consumed in a rapid binge is subsequently expelled as vomit or diarrhoea it is not food alone that is lost from the intestines or stomach. The body also loses gastric juice or intestinal secretions. Gastric juice is more acid that other body fluids, various intestinal digestive enzymes are more alkaline. To compensate for the losses of those charged particles (ions) which account for the acidity or alkalinity of the secretions, the body has to move other particles from one fluid compartment to another. The end result, after a sequence of complex chemical shifts, can be a net loss in the body's store of potassium ions. This may show up, when the blood electrolytes are measured, as a lower than normal level of potassium ions in the blood; a state known as hypokalaemia. The seriousness of this condition will not be appreciated unless the reader already knows that nerve and muscle cells can only function normally when the blood and tissue fluid around them contain normal concentrations of potassium ions. Low levels of potassium can cause nerve fibres to have difficulty in conducting impulses and muscle cells to be unable to go on contracting. Markedly low levels of potassium in the blood are associated with various degrees of muscle weakness in the affected patient. If this state develops it is important that it is corrected quickly; either by taking potassium chloride tablets regularly, or by an intravenous infusion of the appropriate amount of potassium-containing fluid of a safe concentration.

The medical worry is that not all muscle groups develop the same degrees of weakness at the same time. If the heart muscle is the first major collection of muscle fibres to exhibit a failure of function the results can be lethal. (The patient could just drop dead.) We have seen patients whose leg muscles suddenly fail and who literally could not mount the step on the bus although they had had no trouble in walking to the bus-stop a few minutes earlier. Complaints of unexpected bodily fatigue or of sensations like pins and needles in the limbs or around the mouth make it worth while to check the levels of electrolytes in the circulating blood.

Another complication which affects only those who vomit regularly for many months is a dental one. The enamel on human teeth resists the attack of acid gastric juice but is not absolutely impervious to its action. Repeated exposure to stomach acid does in the end dissolve tooth enamel. Those central teeth which receive the full impact of the stream of vomit are worse affected than teeth at the side of the mouth. Incisors (the flat chisel-like front teeth) suffer worst and usually teeth in the top row are affected more severely than those at the bottom. The sufferer first notices that his or her teeth are becoming increasingly sensitive to hot and cold foods. As time goes on the teeth give pain if a draught of cold air goes past them. The dentist will usually crown teeth whose enamel has been eroded in this manner. If the anorexic does not tell the dentist about his or her regular vomiting the dentist may not suspect the condition. In such circumstances the dentist will be very puzzled when the crowns are eroded in their turn too. Even in Britain dental treatment is not free once full-time education is over. Dental charges are high enough for the sheer expense of replacement crowns now and again to be the incentive for someone to stop vomiting because she or he felt that never again would there be enough money for another round of replacement dentistry.

Not only dentists can be baffled by complications arising

from vomiting. There are a number of surgeons who have had young people referred to them with puzzling facial swellings due to enlargement of any or all of the patient's salivary glands. The mechanism which causes these glands to hypertrophy and enlarge is not understood but a small number of patients who vomit several times daily for years do get these swellings, which may make them look like a permanent case of mumps. Some of our patients have had these swollen glands biopsied. The laboratory reports say no abnormality was found in the architecture and cell structure of the excised piece of tissue. No malignant change is present. The surgeon reassures the patient that the swelling is not a cancer or other tumour but himself remains in the dark about why the swelling has developed. No-one breathed a word to him about regular vomiting.

We have found that the presence of such salivary gland enlargement is a reliable sign that the patient vomits regularly. This can be helpful in a thin starver who might not choose to reveal the vomiting part of his or her problem. The facial appearance is in fact at its most bizarre when the vomiter is also emaciated. One girl with swollen salivary glands in the middle of an extremely wasted and skeletal face looked for all the world like an ailing hamster whose cheek pouches remained unnaturally full. The tragedy is that patients can be losing weight and steadily increasing their food restriction while vomiting more and more often and yet find it possible to convince those around them that they are not getting worse because their face does not get any thinner. Wider knowledge of this complication might prevent such mistakes.

Fortunately this complication too tends to right itself once vomiting stops. Even a fortnight without once being sick can produce a noticeable shrinking of swollen parotid glands, though a total return to normal may take many months. Some other workers in Australia have suggested that sometimes the swellings become permanent. We have not ourselves seen this, but the number of people with this problem is only a small percentage of the patients we have seen so we do not feel our experience is sufficient for us to have definite views as yet.

This chapter is about the complications that can set in once the simple 'straight starving' stage has been passed. It is therefore important to point out that the complications of disturbed electrolyte balance, eroded tooth enamel, abdominal distension and enlarged salivary glands that have been discussed so far are complications which affect only some anorexics. There is only one consequence of starting to binge regularly which must affect everyone yet is discussed less often than it deserves to be and that is the financial one. Obviously food costs money so if an anorexic girl suddenly eats a lot more she or her parents will have much higher food bills. In affluent households where the anorexic is still supported by his or her parents these increased costs can usually be absorbed without much more reaction than parental grumbling. By contrast students trying to make ends meet on a tight grant or young people sharing a flat for the first time and trying to make the new wage packet cover all the outgoings can find that the onset of compulsive eating wrecks any chance of balancing the budget. Their increasing overdraft becomes further evidence of personal inadequacy. To those trying to live on unemployment benefit or social security payments the expense of repeated binges can bring financial disaster. If you have spent the week's carefully saved rent money on unwanted food which you then vomit into the lavatory pan, the process doesn't help to increase your self-respect.

The contrast between the thrifty saving which accompanies the starving stage and the apparent financial recklessness which marks the stage of compulsive eating is dramatic and can bewilder parents and spouses. We have known a fifteen year old starving anorexic schoolgirl whose only regular income was the £4 she earned each week from her Saturday job save almost £500 in a two year period. When we worked it out we realised that her total earnings for the hundred weeks she had worked could only have been £400. Not only had she not spent one penny of her earnings for two years but she had also saved every birthday and Christmas present which had come to her in the form of money. As she later recovered she learned how to spend her savings for her own pleasure. At the other extreme was a twenty-year-old sales girl whose repeated binges used up all her earnings as well as an unexpected legacy of £1,000 and still left her with an overdraft of more than £500 at the end of a similar two-year period. Fathers who run their own businesses are perhaps the most upset when they learn of the overdrafts their children have acquired without knowing about the erratic eating which has caused them.

It is easy to underestimate the cost of a single binge. Inflation has altered the figures over the last ten years but as this is written we know that sufferers are this afternoon spending five, seven or even ten pounds on carrier-bagfuls of food which will be consumed this evening and then vomited up before they go exhausted and dispirited to their lonely beds. If you earn £50 or £60 a week you cannot afford to binge at this rate. Even the comparatively better paid anorexics who hold busy jobs which help to control their expenditure (because clearly the demands of being an accountant or a teacher or a junior hospital doctor puts limits on the time available for buying food and then subsequently shovelling it into your mouth) still find it difficult to avoid getting overdrawn at the bank. Their colleagues acquire cars and take out mortgages but their bulimic behaviour keeps these professionals too poor for such acquisitions. (Their friends wonder why they have not money to spend.)

The unemployed are perhaps the worst off of all. They have all day in which to binge and absolutely no money to spare for bingeing. In the end they may eat, all day long, food which they know they cannot afford and which literally makes them sick. The next binge can be triggered by the despair engendered by contemplating the consequent financial mess. Every time they go through the self-degrading ritual their indebtedness gets worse. The misery they feel at being unable to repay the money they have borrowed makes them avoid their friends. With more time to spend on their own the number and duration of binges increases. More and longer binges cost even more money and so the vicious spiral gets another downward twist.

University students who do not have a very full timetable of lectures and classes can find their unoccupied hours degenerate into a lonely prowl round all the food shops and take-away eating establishments near their university. Not everyone eats their junk food at home. Some do it wandering the streets, and then find time to vomit in a public toilet before abandoning their last lecture of the day because they cannot face meeting their fellow students in their reduced and demoralised state. Cutting classes or lectures usually results in falling behind the other students so fear of academic failure then becomes another cause for self-hatred and misery. A binge may then become the only way of blotting out the whole hideous muddle – because at least for the actual moments when the sufferer is shovelling food into herself she is oblivious of everything except the food in her hands and in her mouth. When the binge is over and awareness of the rest of her life returns the wretchedness of the impact of these thoughts and feelings cannot be overestimated. This is the moment above all others when suicide may be attempted. It is not only overdoses of whatever pills may be to hand which are tried. Desperate young women may bang their heads against the door, rub their hands or arms against rough brick walls until their skin is raw and bleeding, cut patterns into the skin on their arms or legs with razor blades or seriously slash their wrists so that bleeding endangers their life.

Self-harming behaviour is hardly ever seen in an acutely starving anorexic. The very few people who precariously achieve a balanced and chronic state of stable starvation may hurt themselves in the depression that follows years of continuous starving, but their self-harm is usually a determined and well-planned overdose with clear suicidal intent, and not an attack on skin and flesh. The few who become self-cutters, and those rare others who hammer their wrists with rocks until disabling bruising has been produced or who stub out cigarettes on their thighs or pour boiling water over their arms have learnt that the physical pain produced by cutting themselves or by the blows or the burns put an end for the time being to the intolerable mental, spiritual and emotional distress which they do not know how to bear. The shock of the physical pain somehow limits the hurting process to the affected limb only and the person's self is made to gather its forces and powers together again in order to cope with staunching the blood flow or getting the burns dressed. The need to cope practically with the self-inflicted injury somehow gets the sufferer out of the abyss of self-hatred which she felt threatened the disintegration of her whole personality. The emotional turmoil she had undergone had produced a tension which she thought would cause her irretrievable and final breakdown.

For the few who turn to self-injury it seems a safer option than 'going to pieces', a threat which can be variously interpreted. Many bingers fear going irretrievably and conclusively mad, though often without having any precise idea of what they mean

by 'mad'. The idea they convey is that they will undergo a
change which will ensure they never recover their former selves
– they will become zombies, lose their identity, extinguish for
ever their individual vital spark. Even girls who have been
helped to emerge from severely suicidal patches by admission to
mental hospital and antidepressant treatment will sometimes,
maybe even after receiving electrical shock treatment and
perceiving it as helpful to them, still express fears that they
might 'go mad' or have 'a real nervous breakdown'. For them
being a patient in a mental hospital and receiving psychiatric
treatment is a different kind of experience from what they mean
by nervous breakdown or going mad.

One of us (J.W.) feels that what is thus confusingly referred to
is in all probability something which could be more clearly
expressed as a fear of losing the sense of who you are. Alternative
ways of saying the same thing which have been used to us
include 'a fear of becoming totally strange to myself' or 'getting
to a stage when I cannot predict what I will do or feel'. This
would match up very precisely with one chronic starver's self
description of her state as 'a structure of facades constructed to
hide a central hole of non-being'. She felt she had no real self, no
actual 'me' with which to make decisions.

This is a topic which we can only touch upon here. We will
return to it in Chapter 7 when perhaps those readers who at
present are confused may find that a second approach to this
central topic of how anorexics experience their own existence
will yield increased comprehension and greater clarity.

Our clinical practice in Bristol has produced about 12 per
cent of very mild and another 12 per cent of moderate to severe
self-harmers among all varieties of anorexics we see. We do
wonder whether those few bulimic anorexics who either place
too low a value on their worth to be able to decline the advances
of any amorous male or who are so scared of bingeing if they
remain alone at night that they would rather have sex with a
relative stranger in order that he should stay in their bed until
morning ought to be included in the group of self-harmers. Are
they in fact practising another kind of self-degradation when
they fail to employ any contraceptive measures during these
connections? Pregnancies begun in these circumstances usually
end in terminations on medical grounds. The experience of

hospital abortion seems like another form of hurting oneself, and one or two patients have put themselves into this situation more than once.

Some readers who may have been led to believe that anorexics are always sexually inactive could be startled by this reference to some bulimic girls having sex with a series of casual partners. And yet a little reflection will surely lead the reader to appreciate that anything and anybody can seem better company than one's own dreary and self-denigrating thoughts, which are bound to follow the inescapable binge if the evening is spent alone. If you don't believe anyone could actually enjoy your company, and if you are also sure that what you say is always boring to other people then it may almost become an obligation to repay the tedium that your escort for the evening must have endured at your hands by at least letting him have access to your worthless and hated body before he goes. If you sleep with him he might even stay till morning. As one girl said, 'You care who uses your best linen handkerchiefs but no-one fusses about who picks up and uses the floor cloth. Once you feel you are that dirty anyone is welcome to have a go, assuming that is, anyone is daft enough to want you!' This attitude does not prevent next day's self-blame for having made yourself cheap but this style of behaviour too can become a self-defeating repeating pattern which is very hard to break. Cessation means facing the loneliness again and the loneliness increases the chances of bingeing.

Similar desperation has led some anorexics to use alcohol or drugs to blur and soften their misery. Regular and excessive use of alcohol by anorexics is less frequent than the occurrence of alcoholism and alcohol-related problems in the general population, but when an anorexic does turn to drink the combined assault on the body's constitution produces a much more rapid downhill course. It is difficult to know where to start trying to achieve some change in these cases. Usually the effects of the dependence on drink makes the doubly afflicted anorexic an unreliable attender at clinics and a poor keeper of appointments so that treatment becomes that much more difficult. Nevertheless recoveries have been made from the double problem but the essential first step seems to be the 'drying-out' from alcohol. A clearly functioning brain seems to be an absolutely necessary requirement for thinking how to combat one's own anorexic leanings and habits.

In our Bristol survey of almost eighty patients first seen between 1973 and 1978 eight at some time had a drug problem. Only one was in the poor outcome category at the end of the follow-up period and she was still using excessive amounts of pain killers to cope with the pain from the kidney stones she had developed as a complication of her anorexia nervosa.

The two girls who had developed a serious heroin problem during their anorexic years were found at follow-up to have discontinued all use of illegal drugs. They were surprisingly the two drug users who were judged to fall into the good outcome category which meant they were leading lives which would not be distinguished from normal on any of the five scales used to measure outcome. The young man who had been on probation for possessing cannabis and the girls who had in turn tried everything from cough medicine to barbiturates, amphetamines to morphine were also no longer using drugs and at the time of follow-up had both been in full-time work for more than a year while their body weights had returned to normal. Like the other three users of mixed drugs they still worried about their weight more than half the time and they all had problems making friends and coping with their family relationships so the state of these five was judged to be only the intermediate one we called improved. These results have been quoted in full because most doctors have very little expectation of real change in their patients when the problem is one of drug addiction or dependence. The results from the small sample in our survey would suggest that such pessimism is not warranted if the drug problem arose in association with anorexia nervosa. In this connection the anorexic hyperachieving tendency, their willingness to try and try again, their drive for eventual success seems to provide the necessary extra ounce of motivation to kick the drug habit and they succeed in breaking free where others fail.

It takes longer to get clear of anorexic difficulties but for these young people their success in breaking free from drug abuse habit seemed to boost their confidence enough to tackle their formerly intractable anorexia nervosa.

The final distressing and humiliating behaviour which anorexics can develop may follow from financial distress or it may arise out of a desperate need for love or simply be a cry for help. Taking what does not belong to you can first appear as an inability to eat food unless the food is actually intended for others. To us 'stealing' does not seem an appropriate description of this behaviour but it is the word used in most sufferers' self-reproaches when they start on this road. Anorexic mothers take bites from their children's sandwiches or eat just the end of the sausage from the child's hot dog but they cannot serve a meal for themselves. They live on their surreptitious pickings from the family's plates. Anorexic nurses may eat food from the patients' dinner trolleys and hastily gobble what the sick patient leaves untouched although hospital rules clearly forbid the practice. Visitors' grapes and boxes of chocolates left on lockers become a torment to them. Anorexic nannies rifle their employers' breadbin and pick at their cheese or raid their biscuit barrel. More drastic is the situation of the girl who drinks cream from the carton in the supermarket so openly that no-one seems to register what they are seeing. Her anti-social action passes unremarked and tomorrow she does it again. A bit more likely to be prosecuted for shoplifting is the anorexic whose rules do not allow her to spend money on food for herself and so she can only eat what she begs, borrows or steals. The constant repetition of her raids on local shops brings detection in the end.

Other anorexics succumb to the urge to take items besides food. Sometimes it is possible to imagine that there is an easily discernible reason for the anorexic's stealing of various items of eye make-up along with the cosmetic lotions which promise a new and glamorous face. Is she stealing the chance of transforming herself into 'the new and lovelier you' promised by the product's advertising? Was the anorexic wife who stole new double-bed-sized sheets subconsciously wishing to renovate the marital bed before she moved back from the single bed in the spare room? Other thefts seem more inexplicable. To steal new sandals the day after a similar pair had been bought in the same shop and paid for in cash by the anorexic girl herself seems an action curiously hard to explain unless she was trying to be caught in order that she could at last tell someone about her problem. For the families of anorexics who shoplift or steal money from the family purse, theft is perhaps the hardest of all things to understand. Once caught and charged with the offence by the police the nightmare of a further humiliating episode hangs over every future visit to the shops. Some husbands have reacted by taking over all future shopping themselves.

In fact the authors are more often puzzled at the number of times anorexics fail to be detected while they are shoplifting. It seems there is sometimes a lack of furtiveness about the action of impulse-ridden anorexics which may protect them from arousing any suspicion in the shop assistants. Sometimes it is only the shock of being caught that can break this behaviour pattern. Once or twice an anorexic in her thirties has sought help for the first time ever in her long-standing illness simply because she was terrified of having to appear in court on a shoplifting charge. It is not only from shops that things are taken. Money can be removed surreptitiously from mother's purse or granny's handbag to pay for the next binge. Repeated thefts of money in the family are hard to handle because of the mutual distrust they provoke. Hushing things up is a natural response but it is not one that ends the problem.

Credit cards can be used with such disregard for the impossibility of paying off the debts incurred that the bank may refer the case to the police. Many bulimic anorexics take a long time to discover the relief and consequent practical help that can result from confessing their problem to their bank manager. It seems to follow that the more secrecy there is about the whole related set of financial and eating difficulties then the worse that sufferer's shoplifting or debt problem is likely to get.

In ten years in our Bristol clinic only three charges of stealing goods from a shop have actually got as far as a court hearing and in each case the magistrates made a probation order with a condition of psychiatric treatment.

For one girl this proved to be the way in which she was at last put in touch with psychiatric help which she could accept. This was after more than seven years of secret binges, constant vomiting, social isolation and financial distress which had several times landed her in hospital after yet one more suicide attempt.

We cannot therefore entirely share the view usually held by relatives that a prosecution is a disaster to be avoided at all costs. An arrest and eventual caution or charge is always a distressing occurrence but sometimes the arrest can provide the crisis which forces a change for the better. It is the unmarked, uneventful road which continues straight on for ever in the same direction without any chance of turning off that offers no opportunity for change. A crisis can be a crossroads and once the difficult corner is turned the new direction can lead around to recovery.

If we always try to use every crisis to promote change and growth we can see them as holding out opportunities for testing new responses. The danger comes when everyone reacts to a crisis in ways that are intended to put everything back just as it was before. If the situation wasn't satisfactory before the crisis why work so hard to re-establish exactly the same kinds of unsatisfactoriness that existed before? They had been proven not to work. A change could be for the better: it is unlikely to make things much worse!

5 External Intervention and How It Can Go Wrong

A few of those who have come to suffer from fully developed anorexia nervosa may still readily accept appropriate help from professional sources if it is offered to them. Now and again the occasional one has even begun the search to locate and contact such help completely on his or her own initiative. In our experience it is far more common for someone *other* than the patient to seek ever more urgently for a professional who knows about anorexia nervosa and who might be willing to help the particular sufferer whose welfare is of such close concern to the persistent seeker. Parents and sisters, husbands or flatmates who manage to find a likely professional source of help then face the daunting double task of convincing the patient that seeking help is something she needs to do now *and* persuading her to make at least one initial visit to the potential helper. The concerned member of the family or the worried friends are obliged to pressure or coerce the reluctant and sometimes angry sufferer to attend an interview which she herself regards as one liable to violate her privacy or to encroach upon her treasured and hard-won autonomy in the realms of food or weight. 'Why should I go? I can look after myself. There's nothing wrong with my weight. Why do you have to *fuss* so much?' would be the usual kind of response from a younger anorexic to a parent who has at last arranged an appointment with an understanding GP or psychotherapist.

The process of getting the sick girl to that vital first interview is often a long one. It nearly always involves confrontations and declarations of feeling which are difficult and painful for all concerned.

What is most likely to succeed in getting the anorexic to accept that (however reluctantly) she must go and see someone about her problem takes place when the people doing the persuading enlist the sufferer's help in assisting *them* to cope with the now-uncontrollable problem of *their* anxiety about her. The kind of persuasion used might be something like this. 'I'm so worried about you that I can't sleep nowadays – I'd feel so much less anxious if you would let the doctor look at you. Then we'd all know if I was worrying unnecessarily. He's got a free appointment on Thursday at 4.0 pm.'

Useful alternative strategies are not plentiful. An authoritarian insistence or an angry and blaming scolding approach may achieve the girl's bodily presence in the clinic or surgery on the appointed day but the chances of her hearing what the therapist has to say with any useful understanding are distinctly lessened if she's been told: 'Once we get you to the doctor my girl, he'll tell you how stupid you've been. He'll make you toe the line and drop all this ridiculous nonsense about being too fat. You'll be in hospital before the day is out – just you see'. Preparation of this kind creates the worst possible climate in which attempts to initiate useful therapy can be tried.

The greater the tensions existing between all those concerned as they arrive in the clinic for their first encounter with the unknown professional helpers the greater the anxiety about the outcome. When so much effort has been used to get the anorexic to the clinic and so much pain has been inflicted, so many tears have been shed, so many exhausting arguments have been endured, the greater the family's need for some useful result from this first visit.

To go through all this painful family dissension and apprehensive waiting for 'the day', only to find that the doctor says, 'Don't worry, it's only a phase, she'll grow out of it', is one of the two worst possible outcomes for the concerned relatives. The other possibly disastrous result will occur if the therapist fails to make real contact with the frightened and self-devaluing sufferer who is hiding behind a suspicious and hostile front. After he has been defeated by anything from passive but polite non-compliance to actively scornful or angry remarks he may emerge to tell the parents that their daughter certainly has a serious problem but he can do nothing to help their child until she actually *wants* help for herself. No suggestions are usually offered as to how this desirable revolution in their daughter's thinking is to be brought about.

The anorexic will of course leave the doctor feeling she has won at least a breathing space if not the whole war. It will be an appreciable time before the exhausted parents who have received messages like the above can pluck up their courage to try and engage help again. Even when the least damaging arguments have got the sufferer to the clinic and she has met a doctor who is willing to tackle her reluctance to consider changing, it is still true that the more the anorexic regards herself as attending 'under sub-poena' rather than as a partly willing collaborator the less likely she is to agree to any of the therapist's suggestions. If attending wholly 'under duress' she will not feel obliged to provide any explanation of her eating habits; nor of anything else either.

The first meeting between the anorexic and the would-be-helper is therefore never easy. This will be true whatever the style of the therapist's approach. If the questions and arguments used by the would-be-helper professional in this first meeting are experienced by the anorexic as aggressive acts which not only threaten her conduct in regard to how much food she eats but also seem to question her entire value system which is centred on the need for control, then this first interview will almost certainly be the last. Yet again the disaster the family rightly fears will have occurred. Why should they trouble to get her to the doctor if nothing useful happens when they get there? A negative result from a first interview is perhaps the biggest hazard encountered when trying to get help for a sufferer.

It takes so much more courage on everyone's part to try again after a negative outcome to one's first attempt. This is why the therapist who hopes to be able to start useful negotiations with the anorexic needs to know the extent of everyone's prior negative feelings in order to lay sound foundations for making sensitive and sympathetic contact with what is almost certain to be a frightened and unhappy person. It is useful, therefore, to ask her who arranged the appointment and who wanted her to keep it and what, having eventually got there, her expectations of the outcome may be. Having been shown that the therapist did not expect her to want to come, the anorexic, feeling less threatened, may be enabled to see the therapist as someone who could perhaps after all understand and who wants to help by listening as well as by being heard. A dialogue between patient and therapist then becomes a possibility but the positive results at this stage may not be immediately apparent to those whose need for the comfort of instant change exceeds their knowledge and experience of eating disorders. Many people encountering the anorexic phenomenon for the first time are dismayed to learn that the time scale which measures the course of recovery from the illness is considerably more extended than they had expected. This can be true of therapists as well as anorexics and their families.

Undoubtedly the foremost wish of parents and everyone else who cares for a skeletal girl is that her weight should be restored to a safer and healthier level as quickly as possible. Therapists naturally share this wish but, while anxious relatives pin their hopes on the *therapist's* ability to induce weight gain without further delay, the therapist is concerned to find the most effective way of persuading the *anorexic* to permit the re-nourishing of her starving body. There is fundamentally no divergence in the ultimate aims of the therapist and family but when the gravity of the anorexic's physical condition has become so extreme that her life is currently endangered the anxieties of all concerned can mount to a level where there may appear to be a conflict of views.

If the family of an anorexic believe that the doctor in whom they are placing their trust is not fully alive to the dangers of the situation their already high anxiety will increase. Since little of positive use can be achieved in a climate of fear and anxiety the therapist, while recognising and acknowledging the real basis of such fears, must endeavour to lower the tension and induce a measure of calmness and hope.

The anorexic meanwhile may be as distressed as those who care for her but for different reasons. The emaciation, which so alarms 'them', is for her the major solace of her life. The apparent determination of those who are supposed to care most about her to take that solace from her seems incomprehensible. If the mainspring of her being must be destroyed then she too must be destined for destruction.

When, because of the physical condition of the anorexic, the first consultation becomes in effect a discussion of how to react to what is a medical emergency the result may be a decision regarding immediate treatment which may initially relieve the anxieties of those most concerned but which subsequently has a damaging effect on the relationships between everyone involved. In the long term (and anorexia nervosa is often a long-term illness) this damage can extend the arduous recovery period beyond the point where it might otherwise have successfully ended. If the damage to family relationships proves to be beyond repair (and we have known this to happen) everyone involved is left with a sense of failure. A hospital bed for Emily this afternoon may signal Emily's exclusion from the family for a very long time. Because of these considerations the doctor cannot simply tell the family what they must do and what is going to be done for their daughter. The problem cannot be approached in such a spirit of confident authority. Authoritarianism is the antithesis of the approach which we have developed in our own practice. For parents, relatives and sometimes for patients as well, this can be a disappointment. Often they are desperate for competent and effective help. In some cases they may have had to overcome not only considerable personal resistance to the whole idea of contact with the psychiatric services but have also had to contend with even stronger resistance from the anorexic sufferer in the ways we have mentioned. They naturally hope for positive assurances that the result of these efforts will confirm the wisdom of their actions. It is not easy for the therapist to sustain their optimistic trust while simultaneously discouraging the development of false hope, but failure to do so may jeopardise the outcome of treatment.

The therapist's approach to the anorexic individual is similarly difficult and in a sense paradoxical. Although it is essential to avoid a purely authoritarian role, the therapist not only needs to win and sustain the confidence of the sufferer but *must* do so in order that collaboration rather than contention or confrontation becomes the basis and keynote of their work together. To achieve this trust the therapist must aim, from the outset, to convince the anorexic of two things.

The first essential is that the therapist gets across unmistakably to the patient that he or she is not only familiar with the whole range of the various symptoms of anorexia nervosa but also understands, in the fullest sense of that word, the complex and apparently inexplicable complications of feelings which accompany them. Since the reason for what is taking place is not, at that stage, always clear to the sufferer herself insistent questioning at the first encounter in order to establish motives followed by a disputatious approach aimed at demolishing those motives is unlikely to produce in the anorexic the changes which everyone desires. The therapist is more likely to make such change possible if he or she can convince the anorexic that although her behaviour and its consequences are by no means unique the sufferer's own experience of these events is recognised as being intensely personal and completely individual to her, although it can be *understood* by the therapist.

Secondly the anorexic must be persuaded that treatment will be aimed at increasing rather than diminishing her own autonomy. She should not leave the clinic after the first appointment feeling she has encountered an adversary whose aim is to extinguish her initiative and demolish her aspirations. Rather she should feel that unexpectedly she has met someone who could perhaps turn into an ally.

Since by definition anorexics are almost completely devoid of self-esteem it requires a careful approach from the therapist to persuade an anorexic sufferer at the first meeting that she is seen as a worthwhile and interesting person rather than as a case worth treating. If the first meeting takes place when the anorexic is dangerously thin the task is even more demanding. The natural and inescapable anxiety and alarm caused by the patient's extreme condition can interfere with the therapist's concentration. In addition the effects of starvation will inevitably impair the anorexic's ability to communicate or respond. Dangerously thin anorexics need (though they seldom want) to increase their food intake. The problem is how to get them to change their behaviour, and to alter the ideas which determine the starving behaviour.

No one, not even a doctor, can 'take over' any patient's ingestion of food for more than a few days or weeks. The extreme method of feeding patients via naso-gastric tubes or by intravenous infusions can only be used for limited periods of time; eating is something that has to be done every day of a person's life, year in, year out.

When treating someone with anorexia nervosa the therapist therefore has to aim at bringing about a basic change in the patient's attitude to food, weight and eating, among many other issues. Only if there are real changes in underlying attitudes, values and beliefs, will changes in behaviour be sustained after all contact with the therapist has ceased.

The available evidence suggests that hospital regimes which force, coerce or constrain a patient by authoritarian methods into eating sufficient food to regain 'normal' weight before she is allowed to leave hospital, without simultaneously attending to her feelings about herself and her value in the world, only produce weight gain which is not maintained after discharge. If the feelings have remained unchanged the weight will automatically be adjusted to match them. If hospital admission was experienced purely as a 'fattening up' process the situation will be further complicated by the reinforcement of the anorexic's negative attitude towards those who are trying to help. If she still feels that she is no one, has no personality, is not worth anything, she will once more shrink her body to fit her shrivelled idea of what her own self is worth and she will 'never never' go near a doctor again. Therapy in such circumstances is almost impossible since the anorexic has not found anyone whom she can trust with her deepest feelings. It is not surprising that treatment of this sort can result in a girl being readmitted four or five times before she can retain the weight she has been made to gain in hospital.

One girl whom we shall call Vanda described, as a number of others have also done, what treatment for anorexia nervosa can feel like when the patient does not have a trusting relationship with those who are administering it:

One of my most vivid memories of anorexia is feeling that I was constantly being deceived – by being fed 'fattening' things, or tricked into eating, and by being in some way excluded – not being told what was going to happen because it would upset me (which was, of course, true – as I knew very well – and so the dilemma, the feeling of being split in two, was perpetuated). This is the feeling I remember most distinctly for my time in hospital – of being ignored, or subjected to tests and experiments, with no communication or explanation. No wonder I felt alternately angry or desperately guilty at being a 'naughty girl' . . .

These words are echoed and their message confirmed by the independent accounts of many other anorexics, one of whom, Virginia, wrote:

Incidentally, any patient is well aware when her drink has been strengthened with extra food supplements, and if this is done she will lose any faith she has in the staff. One deception will be countered with another and treatment will degenerate into a game of outwitting each other.

With a further comment on the essential mutuality of trust which, by its very nature, cannot be sustained unilaterally, the writer continues:

If her treatment plan needs to be changed, the reasons for changing should be explained to her and the mode of treatment discussed and agreed on. She may feel enough confidence temporarily to be able to agree but may lose her courage later when actually faced with extra food or weight increase. This should not be seen as going back on her word, but shows that she would like the reassurance and explanation repeated.

It will be a very long time before she will be able to remember the reasons for gaining weight and be able to tell herself that it is the right thing to do. It may take years of battling with the illness before she can do this.

To those already familiar with all these aspects of anorexia nervosa, most of what has been said will be merely a statement of the obvious. Those less familiar with the phenomena of eating disorders may feel some understandable impatience with the implicit suggestion that treatment must be laborious to be effective and may often be wearisome. To those who are discouraged by this prospect we can only say that the therapist who accepts from the outset that recovery will probably be a slow process will certainly have times when he or she is pleasantly surprised by its early arrival. If, on the other hand, the concept of anorexia nervosa as a long-term illness is not accepted then therapists and other caring staff will almost as certainly suffer a growing sense of failure and become progressively unequal to the demands made on their patience by the apparently interminable nature of the disease. Once lost, the steadfast optimism so essential in those caring for anorexic patients is almost impossible to recapture; this is another of the hazards of mismanaged interventions.

Such discouragement, or the loss of essential optimism is more likely to occur when treatment is undertaken in hospital units which are not specialised and where staff have, therefore, had little opportunity to acquire the particular nursing skills needed for the successful care of anorexic patients and get little guidance about what to do. In such units a series of different styles of approach are likely to be tried one after another with confusing rapidity. In other special units, where experienced staff are skilled at obtaining results which enable patients to be discharged at a satisfactory weight, the hazards are of a different nature as the following extract from a letter in the correspondence column of the *Guardian* illustrates. The writer's letter was a response to one of the numerous accounts of an anorexic experience which are now such a regular feature in the national press. After describing her own anorexic illness some years previously the correspondent wrote:

Two months' intensive treatment in a London hospital was an indescribably horrific time. In itself it was a time of such torture that the fear of ever having to go through it again is the major incentive in my determination to keep my anorexia under some degree of control. (1 February 1983)

Although in this instance hospital treatment was, apparently, successful in physical terms it seems in the long term to have had little more than a deterrent effect as far as the patient's psyche was concerned. Years after the event she claims no fuller recovery than being determined 'to keep my anorexia under some degree of control' for fear of the 'torture' of hospital treatment. No change or modification in her anorexic thinking and feelings is mentioned, nor does the rest of her letter suggest that any such change was the main aim of her recovery programme. There are other people like this newpaper correspondent who – despite accepting that anorexia nervosa is usually initiated by a particular attitude of mind which they feel is often determined by fashion consciousness – nevertheless see it as primarily a physical problem and therefore quite logically susceptible to a largely physical solution. Their disappointment when a degree of physical improvement is not accompanied by a healthier and happier readjustment of attitudes about food and eating is wholly understandable. Such changes rarely occur by themselves solely in response to increasing weight, especially when the increase is imposed rather than self-determined. In fact it is usual for initial weight increase to make anorexics more unhappy and anxious rather than less.

It is important to realise at this point that, because the first essential task is to get the anorexic to change her mind and alter her habitual anorexic thinking patterns, the word 'treatment' is not the ideal one to describe the process. It tends to make everyone, patients and relatives included, feel that the doctor is going to 'do' something to the patient. (Amputate her anorexia perhaps?) In some fields of medicine this feeling might be appropriate. Surgeons will perform operations on anaesthetised patients; dermatologists will paint skin lesions with unguents or lotions; doctors will take blood tests, order X-rays and write prescriptions for tablets which must be swallowed at set times. When the patient is someone with anorexia nervosa the doctor has to kindle the sufferer's motivation and provide sufficient support, encouragement and guidance to enable the *patient* to make changes in *herself* (or himself).

The coronary care specialist has a similar task when he tries to persuade a man who has already had one heart attack to give up smoking cigarettes. What is involved in these two cases is related more closely to education or persuasion than to the classic model of medical treatment. It is a process which has something in common with the efforts of salesmen to induce customers to buy their products or the attempts of advertising men to promote the cause of one or another political leader or medical charity.

The results of such persuasive education, or re-education, in the field of health care should, if they are effective, continue after the process of persuasion has ceased. A coronary care patient who gives up smoking only to resume it six months later or an anorexic who loses all the weight gained in hospital within a month of leaving the ward are both examples of ineffective re-education. There may have been in each case some short-term results but in the long term the desired behaviour change was not sustained under pressure. When this happens to an anorexic it may be due to a maladaptive response to one or more post-hospital encounters with a sample of the many stressful events which are an inevitable feature of all human life. The anorexic's response to the conflict aroused by the new event may be a relapse into anorexic behaviour in spite of the apparent success of refeeding in hospital.

The effects of a challenging and, for an anorexic, hazardous encounter with a demanding new situation or an unexpected and traumatic event will be worse if it occurs after supportive follow-up has ceased or has been prematurely withdrawn. Although the decision to discontinue regular therapy has sometimes to be taken on practical rather than ideal grounds, and may be determined more by college entry dates or job changes rather than relating only to how far the anorexic has progressed on the road towards recovery, the occasional forced early termination of treatment can be successful and the brief relapses which take place may prove to be no more than temporary setbacks on the road to recovery.

It must, however, be said that for many the struggle to escape again from anorexia nervosa can be as painful and difficult after a major relapse as it was the first time. The second time is often worse. This, together with the inherent risk of minor setbacks escalating into major ones, makes it imperative to guard against the potential hazards which still remain even when normal weight has been restored. In fact we would rather say it is most *particularly* important to keep therapeutic contact for longer when normal weight has been swiftly restored because it is our belief that the recovering anorexics who are most vulnerable to the threat of relapse are those in whom the pace of weight gain has been allowed to overtake the gradual modification of anorexic thinking. The added danger for those whose apparently healthy, more solid appearance no longer proclaims their frailty, as their pathetic starving bodies once did, is that no one will protect them from stresses with which, it will wrongly be assumed, they are ready to cope. Their automatic response to receiving this attitude from other people will be to fall back on the 'old way' of coping, the only one they know they can practise to perfection and which they have as yet only imperfectly unlearnt and to which they have as yet developed no useful alternative. The miseries which often accompany these later phases of eating disorders have already been fully described in Chapter 4, and it is not proposed to enlarge further on them in this chapter which deals with the hazards of intervention; but the danger of binge-vomit complications arising from crises of control do constitute a part of those hazards, and that danger underlines the importance of continuing to provide the necessary support and encouragement until the anorexic is sufficiently confident to meet and master all life's problems in her own way and on her own terms. The therapist cannot relinquish his or her task until this point is reached if the risk of relapse is to be avoided.

It should not be necessary to maintain the frequency or the intensity of the earlier therapy when the illness has reached a less acute stage. Sessions which lasted 40 minutes or more at intervals of one or two weeks will gradually be reduced in stages timed to match the patient's progress until, after six months, a year, or longer if need be, all that the patient asks is the chance of a visit each college vacation or at comparable intervals. The purpose of these widely spaced follow-up interviews is ostensibly to ensure that the anorexic feels supported in the event of a threat or challenge to her newly established confidence. In practice they provide the therapist with a most valuable source of insight into the process of recovery; the anorexic who brings back news of her successes and is able to describe how they have been achieved is like an intrepid explorer recounting fascinating adventures in new territory. The therapist learns much from these debriefings which can be used to help other anorexics about to embark on the final stages of recovery. One explorer's experience can often help another to emerge from the shelter of the therapeutic relationship.

Final discharge should be by mutual consent between therapist and patient. The ideal and most satisfactory dissolution of the relationship between them occurs when the patient decides it is time to stop and the therapist confidently and wholeheartedly concurs. Even after formal discharge it is useful to allow for those occasions when minimal contact with a therapist whom they know, and have learnt by experience that they can trust, can help over an unforeseen problem. Many anorexics find maintaining occasional contact after discharge has a particular value. During the first year at college or in a new job or before there is either a firm engagement to marry or an equally strong reciprocal emotional relationship, the ex-anorexic may encounter one or another of the various hazards of recovery, sometimes several at the same time. If this does happen and she is able easily to contact her therapist she will be able to get the help she needs when she needs it, without having to relinquish the non-anorexic control of her situation and of herself which she has begun to establish with such labour. If she can (without having to surmount barriers of secretaries and unwilling appointment clerks) spend as little time as twenty minutes in contact with someone familiar who knows her strengths well enough to be able to reactivate her confidence in herself she will need nothing more. She will do what has to be done for herself. She will be spared the humiliating ordeal of having to adopt again the submissive posture of the new patient telling an old story to someone she does not know and who does not know her.

It is safer for an anorexic at this stage to avoid falling back into the 'down' position after so much effort has been expended, by her and by those caring for her, to help her out of it. Nothing is calculated to 'put down' anyone more effectively than having to relate to a stranger, albeit a medically qualified stranger, all the sordid details of a recurrence of the eating sickness which were described in the previous chapter. The kinder the doctor the greater the shame. If the doctor is less than kind or disclaims competence and seems anxious to refer the sufferer on to yet another more exalted adviser to whom the tale must be retold, then the girl will begin to wish she had not come at all. All the damaged self-esteem, so laboriously reconstructed during the patient hours of therapy and still only tenuously held together, may be shattered by such an experience with tragic results. If the relapse is merely a setback in a progressive recovery, and if the recovery began within a specific therapeutic relationship, and has been continuing under its beneficial impetus after the cessation of regular therapy, then it seems only sensible for the anorexic to take a fresh draught from the original fountain if that source is still available. Doctors who stay put for five to ten years are a very useful resource.

If on the other hand the help which the patient received during the acute phase of her illness is remembered as 'torture' (the word used in the letter from the newspaper correspondent) there will probably be great reluctance to seek further help at a time of crisis when such help could be successful in preventing recurrence of the symptoms or ameliorating their effects by providing the anorexic with stratagems for dealing with them. No stratagem can be useful however, unless it is accepted and understood by the anorexic and actually tried. Therefore, the process of recommending appropriate measures, which he anorexic can use to help herself, must be persuasive. Explanations should convince the individual anorexic that it is worth doing certain things in a particular way; serving her own meals in an appetising and civilised manner for example or meticulously observing a regular mealtime schedule regardless of her own erratic inclinations about food consumption. Hints on how to survive the aftermath of binges will help only if accepted. The explanations about these and similar matters may need to be repeated and amplified and accompanied by constant reassurances that setbacks do not have to be critical. The written word in the form of a letter or a mutually agreed slogan scribbled down in the doctor's familiar language and handed over in the clinic for later use as a reference and reminder has helped many anorexics to survive the 'dangerous corners' on their road to recovery.

Although the complications which arise when anorexics are learning to live a regular three-meal-a-day life are as predictable as the essential characteristics of anorexia nervosa itself, individual anorexics are not. The experiences, the reactions and the rate and manner of recovery cannot be identical for each one

any more than the circumstances of their separate lives could be
expected to be the same in every respect. The helpful strategies
which they are offered may sometimes be modified or adapted
by an individual to her own particular case. When this is
successful it can provide the therapist with an addition to the
repertoire of useful advice available for sufferers who encounter
similar difficulties.

There are other reasons for advocating the return of a
recovered anorexic to a proven source of help if and when
setbacks are encountered. It is comparatively easy for a therapist
to assess the needs of a patient in a current situation if he or she
already knows not only the patient, the patient's family and
their circumstances but also knows from previous experience
the extent of that particular patient's motivation and ability to
change and adapt and to make use of the kind of help available.
These strengths will already have become familiar to both
sufferer and doctor during therapy and they will have carried
the anorexic some way towards recovery. All that may be
needed now is a rekindling of motivation, or raising of morale.
To offer encouragement and recognition of how far she has
already travelled along the path to liberation may be all that is
required to let her see the way out from her new difficulty.

Because a relapse into anorexic ways means a recurrence of
anorexic thinking it is difficult for the girl who slips back into them
when she is separated from those who knew her during her
illness to do the necessary work inside her head without
someone to whom she feels she can safely talk. Many patients
can incorporate their therapist into their thinking so that they
can ask advice from the therapist they carry 'in their head' or in
their memory. If one who cannot do this risks taking someone
else into her confidence she may be lucky and get the help she
needs but equally she may not. Her new friend may be alarmed
and worried. Nothing will be gained and something may even be
lost – whereas a person, like her therapist, who was with her
during the worst period of her illness can more readily convince
her how far she has travelled since that time and can remind her
of all the positive aspects of her situation which in her anxiety
she has too easily forgotten. At the same time the therapist can
help the anorexic to identify the apparent precipitant of the

crisis and work out calmly and realistically what alternative measures are available to deal with it. The implementation of these alternative measures is a task for the anorexic herself; they concern her personally, how she thinks and feels and how she communicates with and reacts to other people. Only if she wants to find a non-anorexic solution to her problems can the therapist help her by discussion and encouragement. But it is universal that decision-taking remains the greatest problem for all anorexics for a long time after their weight has become near to normal.

There is in fact an essential similarity between what the therapist needs to do in the early and the later stages of the illness. Differences are largely in the degree of intensity or urgency which the current situation may demand. The fundamental principles remain the same. Anorexia nervosa cannot be overcome solely by third-party intervention; it is the sufferer herself who makes a recovery and only if she chooses to do so. She will almost certainly need help from one or more other people but her recovery can equally be hindered by unhelpful intervention. What *not* to do is often far more important than doing the right thing.

It is discouraging for would-be helpers, when they feel their efforts are having a negative effect on an anorexic sufferer, but it is not surprising. Such negative effects occur by accident even when the helpers have the best of intentions. To communicate effectively with an anorexic it is necessary to get past her internal censor, which will block any incoming messages directed at the vulnerable areas in her defences and which will distort (by predictable anorexic misinterpretation) all other comments not aimed at a specific target – though she suspects they may be. The anorexic does not hear words as they are transmitted but as her receiving monitor records them for her.

This anorexic censorship is almost puritanical in its blinkered severity. Nothing is permissible unless it is 'right' in accordance with her own value system. Anything which falls even slightly short of this is not less good but 'bad' and just as there are no degrees of goodness there are none for badness either. 'Not good' means 'totally bad'. Everything which the anorexic sees or hears, and every experience she has, is assimilated and assessed by this rigid system as right or wrong. At the stage of the illness when the patient's consciousness is completely dominated by anorexic thinking she lives in a state of constant anxiety lest a momentary loss of control may lead to the disintegration of the internal defences which guard her anorexic value system.

This system, which has already been mentioned earlier and which is more fully described in Chapter 6, decrees that the anorexic should recognise that her best hope for attaining the highest standards of success lies in one field of endeavour, namely adherence to the rigid rules of her own anorexic life style. Other undertakings will only be successful if the efforts required to attain them can be integrated into the anorexic programme and thus be accorded the status of 'good' or 'right' in the anorexic's terms. Academic goals demanding unlimited hours of study and athletic or physical pursuits with rigorous training programmes will certainly qualify, for the anorexic will believe that failure even in these may follow the breakdown of her anorexic control system. Similarly social activities involving food consumption, hours of time spent in frivolous conversation or watching television are 'bad' because they contribute nothing to the anorexic's rigid programme to which her adherence becomes increasingly obsessional.

At the beginning of this chapter we said that before starting to help her a therapist must first convince an anorexic patient that her problem is understood and that her value as a worthwhile individual is perceived. To continue helping, the therapist faces the further task of establishing honest and purposeful communication with a person who, for the time being, cannot risk allowing themselves the necessary freedom of thought or expression to enter into such a dialogue. Even when her confidence in the therapist does permit the anorexic to talk about herself and her feelings, the uncompromising outlook which sees only polar opposites and nothing in between, results in extreme views about almost everything. These opinions may be irrationally optimistic or suicidally pessimistic but they are rarely valid or accurate because they do not recognise the complex nature of reality.

Nevertheless these ideas are all that the anorexic has to sustain her until she can be persuaded that she could live more happily without them. She is like a tiny inarticulate child who has grasped a dangerous object; he clutches it ever more lovingly and will only relinquish it when a sufficiently compelling substitute is offered. The therapist must succeed in convincing the anorexic that there is an alternative way for her to live and be happy without the terrible restrictions she has imposed on herself. How this is done will depend on individual patients and therapists. The family or other significant people in the patient's life may have an equally important part to play in bringing this about. It may not be easy, it can be distressing and it will take time. How much depends on the rate at which those involved can break free of the positions they have adopted in relation to the anorexic illness which, because of the inflexible nature of anorexia nervosa itself, may be helping to maintain the status quo.

While the anorexic remains convinced that the ruthless control of her body's intake and output is the only area of life in which she can confidently expect to succeed she will continue to exert an equally rigid control on incoming communications as well. She has to guard her system from those who would destroy it.

Her conviction that this is the aim of almost everybody she encounters is confirmed every time they speak to her. Cheerful exclamations such as 'At last, you're putting on a bit of weight, that's great – I'm *so* glad' decoded by her inner censor are heard as: 'You'll soon be almost as fat as me and I couldn't be more happy about that!'

Other comments less specifically related to weight such as 'You're looking so much better, you'll soon be your old self again' are heard as 'You can't change yourself or hide what you really are – you'll soon look as gross outside as you feel inside and everyone will see it *and* we expect you to cope with all your problems – there will be no excuse once you are better.'

All this processing and misinterpreting of what is said to her results in the anorexic feeling that her system – her life-support system – the one endeavour in which she least fears the possibility of failure is under constant threat from external forces.

Because the establishment of her system is the only one of the

anorexic's achievements which owes nothing to the assistance
of anyone but herself and because her anorexic ambitions are
probably the only ones to have been conceived and formulated
by, and for, herself alone she is not unduly surprised when their
realisation is not recognised as a laudable achievement by those
who do not understand her value system. She feels it is unlikely
that they would be as successful as she is even if they did try to
emulate her. Their subconscious acknowledgement of inferiority
in this respect explains, in the anorexic's view, their continued
assaults on her anorexic integrity.

The therapist cannot hope for an immediate and positive
response to the initial efforts to negotiate with a patient who
misinterprets in this way all that is said to her. All that he, or she,
can do is to start hopefully and keep going in a spirit of cautious
optimism which should be conveyed as far as possible to
everyone else concerned including the patient.

Enough has probably been said in this and preceding
chapters to explain why we believe that the therapist who wants
to assist the recovery of anorexic patients needs to be as constant
and predictable as the North Star. The most gratifying
recoveries recorded in our practice have been those which
demanded nothing more than a high degree of persistence and
constancy sustained by a reasonable hope drawn from previous
experience. Perhaps it would be more accurate to say that
nothing *less* than this is demanded of whoever tries to help an
anorexic change her mind. Certainly it is difficult, if not
impossible, to maintain the necessary degree of optimism and
dedication without simultaneously caring about, as well as for,
the patient. It can be the only incentive to sustain the therapist
during the difficult and critical times. If there is no particular
commitment to the patient's ultimate wellbeing apart from
restoration of normal weight the patient will perceive this with
clarity even if it is not said. She may never be motivated to get
better because she will not believe it is possible. (Would you want
to talk to a therapist whose only ambition was to fatten you up
and who didn't like you as a person at all?).

Before anyone can help another person to change their ideas,
and consequently change their behaviour, it is necessary to
know what those ideas are. It is equally important to know how

and why those particular ideas have developed and what their function means to the person who has developed them. This, obviously, is what the anorexic's therapist must do and we will, therefore, look more closely in Chapter 7 at some of the complex feelings of those whose thinking has become typically anorexic. There are many people who, for personal or professional reasons, would like to understand more about anorexic feelings. They become interested for a variety of reasons. They may be parents, relatives, teachers or counsellors of all kinds or they may be none of these. Despite the diversity of this group their common interest leads them to ask similar questions about the root causes of the eating sickness.

Some of these questions can only be answered by considering a wider perspective than the narrow view obtained by focusing on the individual subject even if the field of vision is extended to include the subject's family and other individuals who form part of the social group. Before we return to further consideration of the complexities of anorexic thinking we shall, therefore, in the following chapter look at the wider setting and the social implications of anorexia nervosa. We cannot provide definitive answers to all the questions which are so often asked but we can at least offer for consideration some of our own reflections on the broader issues surrounding the eating sickness which have occurred to us during the course of our experience.

6 The Wider Setting

It is just over one hundred years since anorexia nervosa was given its name and only a little longer since its treatment began to be a subject of serious discussion by doctors.

The changes in the economic and social life of the Western world which were taking place in the late nineteenth century were accompanied by changes in the attitudes and convictions of the men and women who lived and worked through the later stages of the Industrial Revolution. The changes in their expectations, both material and spiritual, may be seen as adaptive responses to the many material and intellectual innovations of the time.

Some of those innovations and the reactions and responses they evoked are relevant to the history of anorexia nervosa and its treatment just as prevailing attitudes in general often affect the particular history of various other illnesses and the ways in which they are regarded. The clinical history of anorexia nervosa may be said to have started at that time when it was recognised and began to be the subject of observations and comment in medical publications.

There is no way of proving whether this recognition and the attention and interest which followed were due to an increase in the incidence of the disorder or to the development of the scope of medical practice which was taking place at that time. This development was reflected in the growth and extension of the range of professional medical associations and their particular journals and publications. We know that anorexia nervosa began to feature in these publications but no firm evidence was offered regarding the frequency of the illness. There was, however, universal agreement that it occurred predominantly in females.

Although the illness was experienced mainly by women it was at that time treated only by men and the earliest formulations about the phenomenon were based on the observations and comments of doctors who were members of what had until then been an entirely male profession. Because the first changes in this exclusiveness coincided with the beginning of the clinical treatment of anorexia nervosa it seems appropriate to consider whether the attitudes towards sex in general of those who were involved in the events of that time had any significance in relation to an illness which was regarded as a peculiarly feminine disorder.

The struggles of the first woman doctors to obtain professional recognition have been mentioned earlier. The story of that struggle is rich in incidents which highlight the ambivalence of those who took part in it. Opinions were sometimes surprising and were sometimes changed in the course of time and in the light of events. Florence Nightingale, with her own battle for professional recognition already won, was initially discouraging about the efforts of Elizabeth Blackwell and the other women pioneers who were trying to study medicine. Only later, when she realised that they shared many of her own aims did she become more sympathetic to their endeavours.

Many members of the British Medical Association, when they became aware of the admission of Elizabeth Garrett Anderson as a fellow member deplored the fact that there had been no grounds on which a qualified woman could be excluded. The rules of the Association were altered to ensure that no more of the growing number of eligible women doctors would gain entry but the esteem in which Doctor Garrett Anderson, the first woman to qualify in Britain, was generally held precluded her expulsion under the new rule.[1] The Obstetrical Society did, however, refuse her application for membership in 1874 solely on the grounds of her sex. Her qualifications were not in doubt. In fact they exceeded those of the existing membership in a significant respect since she was pregnant for the second time when she applied. Her membership of the sex whose physiological function was the Society's chief concern prevented her and the Society from enjoying professional fellowship.

Despite such difficulties an increasing number of women went on to enter various fields of work previously occupied almost exclusively by men. The process was encouraged by those men who saw the achievements of women as a valuable contribution to the general good rather than as a threat to their own supremacy.

Not all were confident enough to sustain this broad view consistently and the enlargement of educational opportunities for women drew adverse reactions from many as the following three passages illustrate. If the spontaneous reaction of those who now read them for the first time could be accurately recorded the results might provide some information about the attitudes which actually prevail today. Such general recording is clearly impossible but it is possible for each individual reader to monitor his or her own immediate reaction to these paragraphs. By doing so he or she may enlarge his knowledge of his own feelings and convictions about the subject.

It is quite evident that many of those who are foremost in their zeal for raising the education and social status of women, have not given proper consideration to the nature of her organisation, and to the demands which its special functions make upon its strength. These are matters which it is not easy to discuss out of a medical journal; but, in view of the importance of the subject at the present stage of the question of female education, it becomes a duty to use plainer language than would otherwise be fitting in a literary journal. The gravity of the subject can hardly be exaggerated . . .

Let it be considered that the period of the real educational strain will commence about the time when, by the development of the sexual system, a great revolution takes place in the body and mind, and an extraordinary expenditure of vital energy is made and will continue through those years after puberty when, by the establishment of periodical functions, a regularly recurring demand is made upon the resources of a constitution that is going though the final stages of its growth and development. The energy of a human body being a definite and not inexhaustible quantity, can it bear, without injury, an excessive mental drain which is so great at that time? Or, will the profit of the one be to the detriment of the other? . . .

If she is to be judged by the same standard as men, and to make their aims her aims, we are certainly bound to say that she labours under an inferiority of constitution by a dispensation which there is no gainsaying. This is a matter of physiology, not a matter of sentiment; it is not a mere question of larger or smaller muscles, but of the energy and power of endurance of the nerve-force which drives the intellectual and muscular machinery; not a question of two bodies and minds that are in equal physical conditions, but of one body and mind capable of sustained and regular hard labour, and of another body and mind which for one quarter of each month during the best years of life is more or less sick and unfit for hard work.

These extracts provide an example of how a man who has achieved eminence in his own field may, if he commands sufficient respect in that field, comment on almost any issue concerning human behaviour as long as he does so in the terms of his own discipline where his eminence can render him secure from challenge.

The article in the *Fortnightly Review* of April 1874 from which the foregoing paragraphs have been quoted was written by Doctor Henry Maudsley.[2] Entitled 'Sex in Mind and Education' it conveys the impression of a man attempting to rationalise his fears of the social processes which he observes taking place by warning of their dangerous physiological consequences. With little evidence to support his arguments he repeats his unfounded assertions with an emphasis amounting at times almost to frenzy as though a demonstration of the force of his own convictions would make up for the deficiencies in his reasoning and persuade the reader to his views. He quotes from Milton (*Paradise Lost*)[3] and from the celebrated Doctor Weir Mitchell. According to the latter, the dire consequences of over-intensive education for women were already a reality in America.[4] Doctor Edward Clarke of Boston, from whose book *Sex in Education* Maudsley also quotes, seemed to agree; so did Doctor N. Allen, a physician who found that increasing numbers of American women were unable to breast feed their babies as a result of excessive education at a critical time in the development of their faculties.

During this time the promotion and establishment of new colleges for women were proceeding in Britain. Miss Buss, the educationalist who later with Miss Beale became joint Head of Cheltenham Ladies College, read Doctor Maudsley's article with concern. She had fears that it might discourage some

parents from allowing their daughters to pursue their education.
She asked Elizabeth Garrett Anderson to respond to the article
and attempt to allay the fears it aroused.

Doctor Garrett Anderson's reply, which appeared the following month, was more lucid and convincing than Doctor
Maudsley's paper had been. She demonstrated the fallacies in
Maudsley's arguments and gave practical information on matters
relating to the physiology of women. She pointed out that no
concern was expressed for housemaids and women who laboured
as hard when menstruating as they did in other weeks of their
cycle. They were not considered to be unfit for hard work for one
quarter of each month. Her style was more factual and more
professional than that of Maudsley which had conveyed echoes
of the ancient taboos and superstitions surrounding menstruation found in primitive cultures. She was also more optimistic
about the effects of scholarship. This must have been reassuring
to any of the readers of the *Fortnightly Review* who had been led
to believe that the higher education of women would be the ruin
of the nation.

In spite of such warnings the changes continued not only in
the field of education but in every part of the social environment.
The catalogue of all the scientific and technological advances in
Europe and America in the years between the 1880s and 1930s
has become something of a cliché. Almost anyone over fifty
today is likely to have been reminded by a grandparent, or even
by a parent, that motor-cars and wireless telegraphy as well as
such concepts as antisepsis and radiation were unknown in
their own early life. We in our turn may emphasise the speed
with which such developments have taken place by telling the
next generation how in our youth all aeroplanes had propellors
and that concepts such as genetic engineering and micro-
technology were as yet unheard of. The equivalent message
which they will relay to the children of the twenty-first century
seems more likely to refer to large scale changes in the total
environment rather than to the social developments and
adaptations which take place within the context of the large
scale events.

The potential dangers which threaten the stability of the
relationship between living organisms and their environment
today are considerably more grave than those which disturbed

Henry Maudsley and Weir Mitchell in 1874. The fear that intellectual activity may impair the function of nursing mothers seems to us almost trivial in comparison with those disastrous possibilities which we have come to recognise in our lifetime and which we shall bequeath to our children. The pollution of the oceans and the atmosphere, over-population of our planet, the depletion of its finite resources and overall the threat of the mushroom cloud, these are more terrifying to contemplate that anything envisaged by our forbears.

Despite these realities many of us retain an ability to conduct our lives as though all was well and ever will be. Presumably the ability to push the fear of certain possibilities to the back of the mind and to proceed as though the future held the confirmation and fulfilment of our most optimistic hopes is necessary for survival. For individuals who feel powerless to alter, much less to determine, the course of cosmic events perhaps the creation of a micro climate of hope is necessary in which to produce and rear their young. When in these circumstances a little unit is formed and begins to expand, it is a chilling reminder of the times we live in that we call this phenomenon the Nuclear Family. It is a reminder also that the concept of the family as the fundamental unit of human social organisation has survived widespread economic and social changes. Family life does continue in spite of the threats to its stability and structure from growing uncertainties in the world outside. These threats can make it difficult for a family to maintain its internal cohesion.

The most evident adaptation made by families in response to external pressures is probably the determination of the size of the completed family. There are innumerable motives and reasons for having children and for encouraging others to have, or not to have, them. It is impossible to assess what proportion of the world's population was born in response to social or political pressure and how many are conceived totally independently of any agency other than the mutual desires of the parents at the material time. Whatever motivation brought each individual into being he or she took no decisive part in the event. Nor can children change or modify the physical environment in which they spend their formative years. When, at last, they are sufficiently mature to order their own lives, the manner in which they do so will have been largely determined by the influences to which they were subjected during those early dependent years, influences over which they had no control and in which they could exercise no choice.

That no single human being has any choice whatsoever in the circumstances of his or her birth and upbringing is a fact which may seem too obvious to be stated. In doing so at this stage of our consideration of the social setting of anorexia nervosa, we are echoing the age old cry of the adolescent: 'I didn't ask to be born.' The statement may be old news for anyone else who hears it and the phrase is hackneyed by centuries of use but, for each one who has ever uttered it, there was a first time when the realisation of its truth was an enlightenment.

The realisation by human beings that from the beginning of their lives they have not been able to make independent choices in matters immediately affecting their own destiny comes sooner or later. For most of us it comes at or around adolescence when the hitherto distant prospect of manhood or womanhood becomes an imminent reality. This stage of development is accompanied by an increased awareness of the expectations associated with the sex to which an individual happens to belong. People cannot choose their own sex nor can it be predetermined for them, though there is some evidence that this may eventually be possible. The only choice available to an individual is to accept it or reject it. One can either fulfil the expectations of the assigned sex role or decline to conform with what is expected.

However well prepared adolescents may be for the attainment of maturity, the transition from the dependent state of childhood to autonomous adult status will, in any culture, make great demands on the young person's capacity to adapt to and accommodate the physical and emotional changes which occur at that time. In social organisations and cultural groups less complex than our Western technological world there are still well defined procedures and rituals, primitive in origin, for every stage of human growth and development. Some of these may appear to us so horrific that we would readily support efforts to bring about their abolition by international agencies; but in countries where traditional customs are retained at least everyone involved knows what to expect. The social imperatives are understood by everyone and one system applies to everyone.

In the West there is no such uniformity. Each group and each family is free to determine their own ethos and what particular parents teach or tell their children is in each case their own business.

We need only reflect for a moment on some of the families we ourselves know well to realise how this freedom increases the complexity of our society. Within everyone's circle of friends and acquaintances there are likely to be a wide range of quite different patterns of family life and child rearing. All the families may use similar living equipment and commodities and buy similar foods but the way they utilise those commodities and the way they cook and enjoy their food, and indeed the whole business of life together, will vary greatly from family to family. To outward appearances a cluster of houses of identical size situated in an exclusively residential area may be distinguishable from each other only by minor variations in style. It might be supposed that each will be occupied by similarly standardised families but the quality of life proceeding inside each one will be varied and diverse. These differences and their effects will eventually be reflected in the attitudes and the adaptive responses of the children who emerge from the houses to meet and mingle in school and university. Initially the children may seem to be as standardised as their houses but it will not be long before the ways in which they differ become apparent.

Perhaps the most significant variation in attitudes is to be found in relation to the role of the sexes where the differences are multi-dimensional. Boys and girls differ in their expectations of themselves and of each other. Their parents, from whom the childrens' attitudes are derived, have different expectations for each sex of child. The way these attitudes are manifested may differ greatly between family and family. In addition, society at large is equally divided in its expectations of the sexes though the Role of Women is more often the focus of discussion and comments than the Role of Men.

Although in most Western countries educational opportunities are in principle equally available to both sexes there are still inequalities in practice, particularly in the field of higher education which is more competitive than basic statutory schooling. Everyone goes to school as a matter of course but the right to go to college cannot be assumed, it must be achieved.

This achievement demands a concentration of effort from adolescents and young adults at the period of their lives when they are simultaneously adjusting to all the other changes associated with the growth into manhood or womanhood. It is a critical stage of their development. It is also the time when the beginnings of anorexia nervosa most frequently occur. Because these facts are well known and because many more girls than boys are known to become anorexic the causal explanations for the condition's existence sometimes rely on the fact that sufferers tend to be emergent females rather than emergent males as though this alone were a sufficient basis from which to draw conclusions about the phenomenon.

The idea that anorexia nervosa in emergent females may be a response to the threat of womanhood has been convincingly argued in specific instances. It cannot, in our experience, be made to fit every case and seems, therefore, to be incomplete rather than totally wrong. It presents difficulties in the case of the male anorexic who must presumably be responding to the threat of emergent manhood. Again this may be partly true but it is unlikely to be the whole story. These difficulties illustrate why it is necessary to see the eating sickness in a wider context and to look first for answers to general questions and relate these to more specific ones about particular cases.

Two general questions are relevant. The first one is why are no cases of anorexia nervosa reported from the poorer non-industrialised countries?[5] The second concerns the possible reasons for the apparently increasing incidence in the industrial West. The answers to these two general questions hold the key to some specific ones, which are asked by many who seek to understand anorexia nervosa. These questions are usually: Why more girls than boys? Why more often at adolescence than at other times? And why more frequently in what may be colloquially termed 'well-to-do' families rather than in those less well off?

Clearly the last question relates to the first general one. Families in Third World countries where the majority of the population is wholly engaged in a daily struggle for survival are unlikely to have children who can be candidates for higher education and so enter the group which has a high risk of developing anorexia nervosa. The same is true to a lesser degree in the lower income groups in the West. It is possible that a clever child from a poorer family may succeed in realising his or her full academic potential but statistically the chances are worse than those for a child whose parents are professionals. Anorexia nervosa does occur in the children of families from lower income groups but it does not happen very often. There is therefore a connection between socio-economic status and the eating sickness which seems likely to have some relevance to the frequency with which the condition occurs among university students and others whose education continues beyond the statutory minimum school leaving age.

The majority of families whose children go to universities are likely to be living at a level of affluence well above the base line at which the struggle for the satisfaction of basic needs is paramount. To what extent the memory of that basic struggle remains part of the collective consciousness of the family will depend on how far back in the history of the family it took place. Increasing upward social mobility in the population generally has resulted in an ever-increasing group of families who have attained economic stability and safety a very short time ago.

The struggle, whenever it takes place, is likely to have been won by the time the children start college or university; but the economic stability of any family may be threatened by external events at any time. This ever present possibility, like the global problems to which it is frequently related, may contaminate and destabilise the micro-climate of those families most susceptible to its influence. The most worried about the possibility of failing to maintain their position will always be those who have most recently attained it and who have had little time to establish themselves in their new status. How does a family in such circumstances maintain its own stability? How can an equilibrium be sustained which will allow each member of the family to have an equal chance of life, liberty and the pursuit of happiness when the ability to achieve an above-average living standard can be seen to have been attained?

At this stage there may be still resources of energy and potential for further achievement within the family which will demand an outlet for fulfilment. There may well be a sense of greater things to come. Even among idealistic families whose explicit values are avowedly anti-materialistic it is difficult to find more than a tiny minority who would willingly revert to a lifestyle of poverty for themselves and their children in the conviction that it was the only proper way to live. There is more likely to be a dynamic thrust of achievement leading to further achievement which can help to counteract the dangers which adverse external events present. There is always the hope that the children's achievements will add to the security of the family as well as ensuring the children's own futures. Highly successful offspring may enhance the stability of their families as much as children with multiple problems may threaten it. The responsibilities of adolescents in families which have a pattern of achieving are therefore considerable. The more recent the parental achievements the greater the risk of the adolescent being unable to fulfil these responsibilities to the standard they perceive as the norm for their family and which they assume to apply to themselves.

In countries where educational opportunities are limited, and where family life is still largely regulated by cultural conventions, the failure of a young adult to meet the requirements of that culture would be unlikely to affect his or her family to the same extent as in the industrialised West. The answer to our second question – Why does the incidence of anorexia nervosa seem to be increasing? – seems, therefore, to lie in the probability that in some parts of the world there is a proportional increase of what we know to be the high-risk categories for the condition in the population.

We have considered two of the specific questions which are commonly asked about the occurrence of anorexia nervosa, namely, why it usually starts at adolescence and predominantly among the socially and economically established. We should also consider the third specific question which is perhaps the one most often asked. Why more girls than boys?

This is perhaps of the three questions we have raised, the one most closely connected with the subjective feelings of the people concerned. This may explain why some commentators who recognise the essentially subjective nature of the eating sickness tend to focus their attention on the sufferers' attitudes towards their own sexuality. There are several reasons why an approach which relies entirely on the notion of rejection of the sex role may limit the understanding of anorexia nervosa. One difficulty which has already been mentioned is that the theory applies less convincingly to male anorexics. It is also deficient when applied to females who develop the condition after they have already accepted their sex role and fullfilled it in relationships including marriage and motherhood.

Another danger is that over-reliance on one particular aspect of maturation may result in underestimating the importance of other aspects which are of significance to the male sex as well.

The important physical and emotional changes of adolescence are accompanied, for both sexes, by the challenge of exposure to a range of hitherto unencountered intellectual and moral influences. These influences and ideas may differ from, or even be radically opposed to, those which prevailed at home during the formative years of childhood and which are unlikely to have altered substantially during the comparatively short period covering the transition from child to young adult. Although for the adolescent the whole world may seem to change between sixteen and eighteen, for parents the same two years covering perhaps the ages of forty-four to forty-six or thereabouts are not normally associated with intellectual expansion and emotional intensity on a scale to match their children's experience.

Parents who recognise that their children's development is at a critical stage are likely to take merely a rational view of the process. They are aware that what the children achieve at that period will determine their standard of life in subsequent years. The children or adolescents are no less aware of the immediate situation but their appreciation of it is more influenced by emotion than is that of their parents. For the young people now is when you live and it is the only time. Renouncement of a certain joy today will not be compensated for by a substitute satisfaction, designed to the parents' specification, tomorrow or in ten years time. Their parents' hopes for them may not even coincide with their own aspirations for themselves. While adolescents are preoccupied with nonrational and nonmaterial considerations their parents are, understandably, concerned with the necessity to plan for future economic security, the need to have a career.

To the emerging adult of both sexes this emphasis seems to devalue and even totally discount the importance of emotional values. Even intellectual satisfactions, the realisation of which is for many one of the new found delights of adolescence, often appear to be regarded merely as a useful way of getting ahead of other competitors in the rat-race who have no such qualifications. This conflict between the demands of the rational adult world and the instinctive and imaginative impulses of the newly matured adult is experienced by both sexes but it may well be true that for some girls the conflict cuts deeper than for any boy. This may be why those girls who, while struggling to resolve the conflict, succumb to an eating sickness are thought to be rejecting womanhood. The following extract from a letter written by Petra when she was recovering fom anorexia, describes this conflict and suggests why its resolution may be harder for a girl than it is for a boy. In the following extracts Petra and Marcia are real former patients of ours though their families do not know them by these names and it is we who christened Petra's fiancé Bernard. The writer of the later extract from Anorexic Aid's *News Sheet* also exists in the real, not the fictional world:

I often feel that changing jobs so often is to try and run away from Anorexia and its effects, but I seem to forget it's within me. No doubt standing up to it and punching it on the nose would be far better, but I have never been good at standing up for myself, or getting into an argument which would solve things far quicker. I tend to sulk or let comments fester in my mind to outsize proportions. I seem to have to be permanently occupied in constructive jobs of my own seeking – preferably not be told to do a job as it is then a chore. I love housekeeping and resent the fact that it is necessary to have a job! Society points out that we have to work and yet all I want is to get married to Bernard, have his children, keep house, and yet that sets up a conflict in me with the things that you are brought up and taught. I find if I am physically active I feel much better, but it gets hard to do that once you've let yourself slide. It's the feeling of how dirty you are inside that makes you feel it must show outside, which may account for the fact I'm not happy unless I am slim enough to see my bones, 'the real me'. It worries me that I may find once I'm married 'routine' could unbalance me, and the fact Bernard doesn't know about it could make me more devious rather than fighting back at it so it doesn't rear its frightening head.

Petra knows what she wants to be and do and, far from rejecting womanhood she longs for the chance to fulfil it if only she could reconcile her own inclinations with what she believes are the demands of 'Society'. She might, at an earlier stage of her illness, have been less clear about her own objectives but her confusion was more likely to have been due primarily to her effort to meet external demands rather than solely to any suppression of internal inclinations.

Marcia, who wrote the following words in a letter to the authors, was also recovering and though she has different aspirations from Petra she expresses herself with the same defenceless openness which is characteristic of so many sufferers from the sickness, (*once they have stopped starving* and found someone they can trust to understand their words).

As for the future – well it looks like a mixture to me really. I would like to eventually do the certificate course to become a field social worker as I feel pretty stunted at present . . . However I realise that this is only a move to make me feel better and more worthwhile to myself, and also that I *always* mess up anything which is going to be advantageous to my own perception of myself, so even if I were accepted I would probably, in my present frame of mind, find a way to fail. However I keep hoping. Otherwise it's pretty gloomy I'm afraid. Scared of getting old, losing my looks, having nothing else to offer except youthful femininity, and when that goes . . . Well! Also lots of regrets – for the first time I feel sad about not living my life in a different way, having wasted so much time, and for it to be too late for so much. (I think I cherish the illusion that if I'd been different I would by now be a combination of Isadora Duncan, Kate Bush, Katherine Hepburn, Picasso and Patrick Lichfield!) I don't think I'll ever be truly at ease with myself until I am a truly creative person and, of course, I lack the courage to explore because I feel I lack (or know I lack) the talent to do it.

You asked if there was anything I would like to say to others who are seeking help for similar problems. Yes lots, and yet not much constructive I'm afraid (forgive me if now I become either very trite or ridiculous!). Anyway – I think everything is tied up with women's perceptions of ourselves as people. We feel we have to be all things to all people, and also to ourselves and we can't do it! (Which is not to say *I* don't keep trying!) Somewhere along the line where others accept not being slim, beautiful, talented, sexy and a true goddess, we can't. (And just one is not enough.) We also tend to form destructive relationships with people who *expect* all these things in one! I can tell other people to ease up on themselves, and to accept themselves as real, but I can't do it for me! Also Society itself is in such a state it can only be expected that people have problems – who knows, as Society becomes more and more complex and ridiculous then it can only produce more fear, more phobias and more odd ways in which stress shows itself. In short, I would like to be rid of this thing, but at present I don't see much hope for any of us.

Although Petra and Marcia each describe different ideal life styles both express similar misgivings about their ability to succeed in the roles which they feel offer them their only chance of happiness. Both share the anorexic diffidence in the way they deny priority to their personal aspirations over the demands of 'Society'; (the capital letter for the word society was used by both writers). This diffidence is so extreme that they barely acknowledge the existence of personal rights for themselves – let alone demand or compete for their attainment.

This subordination of any individual's inclinations, almost to the point where it seems such personal wants never existed, can and does seriously impair that person's confidence in his or her ability to make the 'right' decision in any situation which presents a choice of options. The elimination of the subjective or personal factor robs the choosing process of one of its vital elements. As every careers guidance counsellor knows, most people do best in whatever they undertake when enthusiasm and instinctive commitment are allied to ability. To do well something that is found to be enjoyable for its own sake is one of life's greatest satisfactions. The satisfaction is enhanced when others welcome and value the achievement, but other people's approval and esteem are not enough to compensate for having to work at an uncongenial job. Even if the task is done well it remains a chore and can become a growing burden.

Neither of the two girls whose letters are quoted expressed any confidence in their ability to succeed even if they had been able to allow themselves to follow their own wishes. Both wrote as though they believed that, in a way that is inextricably connected with their eating problems, they were programmed for failure. The letters were written, some considerable time after the most acute phase of the illness had passed, when both girls could be described as almost recovered. The ability which enables them to express clearly what, ideally, they would like to achieve and experience in life is so different from the dutiful striving to meet the demands of others, a characteristic of earlier stages of anorexia nervosa, which were described in Chapter 2. Nevertheless the long years of 'ought' and 'must' can be seen to have taken their toll. It is almost as though to allow 'What *I* would really like' as a basis from which to act would tempt fate into exacting retribution. Others may be free to follow their fancies with impunity, to sing, dance, paint, sail boats or marry 'Mr. Right' and raise children but not the anorexic nor even the ex-anorexic. The punishment for such 'selfishness' might, perhaps, be the thing they fear most in life; it would all be bound to go wrong. They would be doomed to fail.

An anorexic's own assessment of his or her achievement level is often very different from the judgement of more objective observers. Even when the sufferer has acquired a more realistic view of what she can do she still feels that any failure or mistake, however small, will bring disaster. This persistent fear of the consequences if she fails to meet the demands or to measure up to the requirements of a situation is likely to remain for a long time after the eating difficulties have grown smaller. When these performance anxieties are increased through stress the old eating problem may again, to quote Petra, 'rear its frightening head' and no amount of reassurance from others, even the nearest and dearest, can persuade the sufferer that far from being a useless person she is already regarded as a successful one. In her heart of hearts she has always known she is a failure. She fears other people will come to realise it too if she is seen to fail, however slight the actual failure may be.

The sense of living under the constant threat of failure and the way this affects a person who experiences it has been described by another sufferer. The following paragraph is from a letter which appeared in the news sheet of the British self-help group Anorexic Aid:

In fact I was denying myself the food I needed as a way of punishing myself for my lack of self-confidence and success in the things I wanted to be successful at. This not eating was one thing at least which I was in full control of in a world where I seemed able to control little else to my advantage, and being thin was one way of proving to myself I could do things for myself.

The writer goes on to say how the help of a specialist counsellor contributed to the restoration of the

Self-respect and self-confidence that were so lacking in my life and whose absenses were my real problems, and I now feel that I am fairly well cured, though I must wait and see whether further unhappiness in my life may lead to a reappearance of anorexia.

The letter ended with a reference to the writer's restored 'zest for life' and a recommendation to other sufferers of the type of counselling which he had found so helpful.

The feelings described by this male anorexic, as well as his attitudes towards food and his eating behaviour, replicate those of hundreds of female sufferers. If it is accepted, as we have suggested earlier, that many of the emotional and intellectual features of adaptation to the changes of adolescence and maturation are common to both sexes, this similarity will come as no surprise.

If many of the feelings about adult life, its responsibilities and the expectations it imposes, are shared by young people of both sexes the unequal occurrence of anorexia nervosa cannot be attributed solely to a characteristic of female biology or psychology. It seems more likely that the pressures and demands of what Petra and Marcia called 'Society' on young women are more confused and internally self-contradictory than the equivalent pressures and demands on young men. The conflicting expectations can overwhelm young females in a way which rarely happens to young males, unless they are sensitised by a severe conflict about their career choice.

Standards of education in Europe and America have developed far beyond anything envisaged by the nineteenth-century doctors who worried about the effects of learning on women's health. Now a girl with ability is not only permitted to compete with her brothers for a place in tertiary education but is expected to do so. The competition will continue and get more severe if she then proceeds to further specialist training and embarks on a professional career.

During this period of striving the adaptations to adult status will be taking place but for each sex the social implications will be different.

Boys or young adult males are generally speaking allowed, even in some instance encouraged, to explore every avenue of experience available to them and to demonstrate to themselves and to others their claim to manhood. They may carry out this process with all the exuberance and enthusiasm characteristic of their age group and incur no penalties. Unlike their sisters they are expected to be assertive and allowed to be aggressive without arousing significant disapproval. If boundaries are overstepped, or toes trodden on, the censorious may be reminded that 'you're only young once' and if the transgressions are particularly amusing or original the reputation of the perpetrator may be enhanced. After all boys will be boys.

In the days before women's emancipation no girls could risk the social consequences of copying their brothers in this overt testing-out of their own assertive or rebellious capacities. Now they are expected not only to match the boys academically but also to be able to share their emotional and physical adventures in the same spirit of youthful freedom. Somehow it is nevertheless still expected that the girls will show adult standards of responsible behaviour with no preparatory learner phase. They carry the burden of seeing things don't go too far. If exploration by a couple results in a pregnancy the division of responsibility is likely to leave the greater share to be assumed by the girl, and this still influences parental actions.

The attitudes are expectations of parents and others towards girls is less clearly defined than when the upbringing of each sex was totally dissimilar. The social changes of today are recognised while many of the social imperatives of yesterday still linger and produce an often unconscious double-standard in parental policy. Daughters are fetched home when sons make their own way back from the party later. The extent to which these ambivalent attitudes and expectations may influence the behaviour and development of adolescents will vary between different families and social groups. It seems to us that we can formulate some general ideas which reflect the views of many parents at least some of the time.

The ideal daughter will be successful in the studies which will open the door to a good career. She is expected to show interest in the opposite sex but not to the detriment of her academic work. She ought to make herself attractive to them but not too conspicuously or with bad taste. On the other hand she must avoid being too clever or she will be unpopular. At family functions her presence is essential. Her absence would be deplored and the importance of her role in the family will be stressed while her brother spends increasing amounts of time elsewhere. When he is at home he is allowed a latitude in the matters of clothes cleanliness, bad language, rough housing with friends and occasional drunkenness which are unthinkable for a girl, for this ideal girl anyway. The ideal boy may still be a favourite son if he achieves few of the things expected of his sister. Provided he has safely started on his career ladder he may rise at noon on Sunday without incurring comment whereas erratic timekeeping in the case of a daughter would be more likely to annoy the parents.

While the maturing boy gradually detaches himself from the family, it is expected that he will do precisely what he is doing, that is, begin to leave home in stages. The ties which linked him to the family home are slowly replaced by others integrating him with a wider world outside it. He meets with approval at every stage of his emancipation. For the girl, at the same point in her development, there is often a different experience. Maturity seems to integrate her further into the family. If she does not help, eyebrows may be raised. More responsibility for its emotional well-being seems to be devolved upon her than on her brother. Because she is far more of a care-giver in the family than he is it becomes more difficult for her to differentiate her own needs from those of other family members. In a family which prides itself on its 'closeness' such differentiation may be impossible and might even be regarded as unnecessary or unwelcome. 'Your son is your son till he takes a wife, your daughter's your daughter the rest of her life.'

Although this stereotype is not an accurate description of every family it is one which, with appropriate modifications, many may recognise. The recognition that adult autonomy is acquired in different ways and to different degrees by boys and by girls and that the acquisition of autonomy by girls gets a more mixed reception from adult observers, provides, we believe, an important part of the explanation of why more girls than boys develop anorexia nervosa.

An intelligent and sensitive young person of either sex may, in the circumstances described in this chapter, agonise over the choice of the 'right' options in life in order to meet the expectations of 'Society's' agents. When the demands of society are confused, and its agents send out conflicting signals, making a 'correct' decision becomes a complex and difficult task. The complexity can be increased when additional demands, specific to a person's particular sex role, conflict with those which are common to both sexes. In the social conditions prevailing today in the industrialised world this extra conflict is more likely to be experienced by girls than by boys. It follows therefore that more girls than boys will lack confidence in their abilities to achieve the goals for which they feel obliged to strive. Those who are haunted by the fear of failure can become vulnerable to anorexia nervosa.

Those who do succumb to the condition believe themselves to have already failed or to be facing a state in which future failure is unavoidable. They find themselves in a closed situation where the best they can do may still not be sufficient to achieve what is expected of them. There seems to be no way out; no alternative solution exists. They feel bound to disappoint those whose hopes they are striving to fulfil. In fighting and overcoming what they regarded as egotism they have subdued their ego. By this self-abnegation they have relinquished or failed to develop their autonomy. By trying to please everybody they have made themselves nobodies. We believe the starving anorexic shrinks her body to fit her diminished or non-existent sense of self.

NOTES

1   Jo Manton, *Elizabeth Garrett Anderson* (London: Methuen, 1965).

2   Doctor Henry Maudsley, 1835–1918. In 1908 the London hospital
     which bears his name was endowed, largely by his efforts, to
     promote and foster research based on the rigorous standards of
     accuracy and comprehension which informed his own work in the
     treatment of mental disorders.

3   John Milton, 1608-74, *Paradise Lost* Book IV Line 297-9:

> For contemplation he and Valour form'd,
> For softness she and sweet attractive grace;
> He for God only, she for God in him.

The first two of these lines were quoted by Doctor Maudsley; the
last was not included.

4   Doctor Silas Weir Mitchell, 1829–1914. A Philadelphia neurolo-
     gist who developed an approach to the treatment of mental
     disorder based on the establishment of a calm, orderly, tension-
     free regime. This required a break from daily contact with
     relatives and others and became widely known as the 'rest cure'.

5   Abua Nwaefuna, 'Anorexia Nervosa in a Developing Country',
     British Journal of Psychiatry, March 1981, vol. 138, p 270. This
     letter describes a case of a twenty-two year old Nigerian woman
     who was treated for severe weight loss following self-imposed diet
     restriction. After refeeding in Lagos University Teaching Hospital
     she lost weight again on discharge, was readmitted and treated by
     hypnosis. The author claimed that this was the second reported
     case of anorexia nervosa in a black patient. The first, to which
     Doctor Nwaefuna referred, was a child who was one of forty-two
     patients in a study at the Presbyterian Hospital in New York. This
     study by M. P. Warren and R. L. Vande Wiele, 'Clinical and
     Metabolic Features of Anorexia Nervosa', *American Journal of
     Obstetrics and Gynaecology*, October 1973, vol. 117, pp. 435-9,
     was concerned with patients in the socio-economic group which
     enabled them to pay for private treatment. It seems probable that
     this also applied to the Nigerian patient.

7 Internal Feelings

Readers of all the chapters which preceded this one should by now be persuaded, if indeed they ever doubted it, that anorexia nervosa is about feelings rather than about food. Nevertheless many people who are already well aware of this want to understand more about the nature of those particular feelings. In this chapter therefore we will return to the consideration of the thoughts and ideas of individual anorexic sufferers which we began in Chapter 5.

It should not be difficult to understand why the anorexic girl as we described her at the end of the last chapter will find it impossible to make even the simplest of choices. The necessity for any kind of decision can arouse in her either panic or despair. Bereft as she has become of any true or reliable sense of her own identity, she is equally indecisive whether the decision relates to trivial details or to matters of great importance.

Where we have had the opportunity to work closely over a long period with any individual on the issue of indecisiveness, we have noticed that an inherited conflict of values passed on to the sufferer by her parents has been an important factor. Typically her father will have shown her by his example how important it is to be independent and think for herself and by her own efforts get ahead and achieve results. During the same formative years her mother will have been teaching her to show consideration for other people and impressing on her how important it is not to be greedy or selfish.

Frequently an anorexic ends up with two ways of being

wrong and no way of being right. The choice between being a doormat who lacks a mind of her own and a selfish person who ignores other people's wishes is not an easy or comfortable one. Most of us who are not anorexic can escape this trap by consulting our central 'core' self which will usually be able to give priority, on a particular occasion and in its surrounding circumstances, to one or other of the conflicting value systems. We can decide that as today is Granny's seventieth birthday it is more appropriate to let her wishes prevail. Tomorrow, when Granny thinks we are unwise to go for a long country walk in the rain leaving her alone all afternoon, we can cheerfully tell her that we will be much better company for her when we've had our tramp in the fresh air with no sense of guilt at having chosen to please ourselves this time.

Even the purchase of basic items of clothing becomes a torture of anxiety. It is not so much a question of not knowing what she wants; she doesn't of course but that is the lesser problem, the major problem is that she does not know what she *ought* to want. For most people need determines choice but what the anorexic may need barely concerns her since she is usually convinced that she deserves and therefore should have – nothing.

Although she cannot deal with this difficulty by evading it altogether she can, at least, try to minimise the number of occasions on which the need to choose arises. She cannot do the same with birthdays, Christmas or other festivities. There is no question of choice and no escape from their inexorable arrival. She cannot escape from presents and the statutory rituals which accompany the giving and receiving of gifts. She must endure an agony of embarrassment as she strives to produce appropriate responses. Her simulated gratitude barely disguises her feelings of unbearable shame. She is not worthy to receive and it was, therefore, 'wrong' that the gift was imposed.

These feelings make it difficult, even impossible, to say a heartfelt 'Thank you'; to accept the present gladly and enjoy it in the way that the donor intended. She cannot even recognise the validity of that intention but changes it to fit her own perception of herself as one who must surely be seen to be unworthy of such a gift. The anorexic's total inability to be casual about anything invests the transaction with an unwarranted portentousness;

the very word 'casual' would be changed in her vocabulary to 'slack' or 'sloppy' and thus become reprehensible.

Communication between giver and receiver is confused as though by a bilateral scrambling device so that it is not only the anorexic who misinterprets what she hears. Her family, unaware that she is 'changing' their messages, are in turn misled by her apparently inappropriate responses to them. These responses may vary between dutiful cheerfulness, a forced and superficial gaiety or a mute and tense withdrawal. Whatever attitude is assumed by the anorexic it is unlikely to be a true reflection of her real feelings. It will also be misunderstood by anyone who is unaware of the extent to which her thinking and behaviour is dominated by her anorexic system. The attempted cheerfulness, if it succeeds, may give rise to false hopes that the anorexic is 'more like herself again' while the tense withdrawal is seen as further confirmation of the familiar complaint 'we used to be so close and now she hardly speaks to us, I can't get through to her at all'.

Even those parents, relatives and friends who do have some perception of what is going on behind the facade which is presented to them are often at a loss to know how to use their insights in the best interest of the anorexic. The importance of an empathic understanding of the individual who is suffering from anorexia, as a prerequisite for understanding and treating the illness itself, has already been stated in Chapter 5 and neither experienced therapists nor anorexic sufferers would challenge this view. Many parents, medical students and other counsellors and helpers who are encountering anorexia nervosa for the first time, are aware of this requirement but quite reasonably ask what next they can do, after gaining understanding, which will be of some help to the sufferer.

Sometimes this question is asked with a degree of impatience which may well be justified. Anorexia nervosa has no endearing qualities and during its course it can inspire negative and unhappy feelings in those whose duty it is to care as well as in those who suffer from it. It is possible for other people to feel, in their anxiety, irritated, critical and sometimes angry with a deliberate self-starver. But although the strength of these feelings may often be disturbing and always distressing to the carers it is unlikely they will ever match the intensity with which anorexics dislike themselves.

In the course of therapy it is helpful if relatives, therapists and friends feel free to vent their irritated and angry feelings at 'this wretched disease' which is damaging the sufferer so badly. It is of course an artificial device to treat the disease as a personified object separate from the patient, but it enables one to sit beside the anorexic sufferer in a close and caring way, which is felt by the patient to be supportive, while saying such things as 'I hate the way this anorexia nervosa has diminished and hurt you and spoilt so much for us. I resent the limitations which it has imposed on your life and ours. I wish it had never got hold of you.' In this way negative feelings can be ventilated safely without being hurled at the patient's head as damaging attributes of *blame* which will only retard progress to recovery. Unless time is found to express irritation in safe ways at relatively calm moments it is inevitable that the most controlled parent or therapist will 'blow his top' at some minor check which proves to be the last straw for his temper; when this happens weeks of good work are undone in a second.

The self which is so abhorrent to the anorexic must, of course, be concealed. Anyone who does manage to discern it is certain to be disgusted by the revelation. The anorexic lives in constant fear of this disclosure. She believes that her inner self is gross, unclean and intemperate and must at all costs be subdued. The ability to do this is usually the only positive attribute which the anorexic can acknowledge though she may sometimes allow herself some satisfaction at the success of her dissembling behaviour.

This behaviour is intended to provide an acceptable false 'front' to camouflage the unacceptable real self behind it. Even when this operation succeeds it is only a hollow victory. An apparently amiable social interaction between the anorexic and another person who seems to be friendly and whose attitude indicates a willingness to extend the relationship between them, whatever its present basis may be, has little chance of making progress. For the anorexic the risks are too great and there is no incentive to persuade her to undertake them. She is too aware that increasing intimacy will lead to the horrifying discovery of her true self by the person she has succeeded in deceiving. If she attempts to continue the relationship by keeping the other person at arm's length while continuing the deceptive process, the strain will be intolerable and the success of her deception will make her feel even more despicable. The more attractive the idea of responding to overtures of friendship the greater these fears will be. The only safe response is one which precludes the possibility of a closer relationship and this is the one which is almost invariably chosen.

The saddest aspect of this is the fact that many anorexics are desperate for human contact, for the warmth and approval and the uncritical acceptance of an ordinary loving relationship such as everyone else seems to take for granted. They need it as much as their undernourished bodies need food but they are unable to take it even when it is offered to them.

The incapacity to sustain personal relationships is not confined to those which are potentially significant. Even quite impersonal and comparatively insignificant encounters can be painful. A neutral question or comment from a librarian, a shop assistant or a fellow student is misinterpreted by the anorexic as a 'put-down' and can reduce her to tears (restrained of course until she can take refuge in seclusion). However bland or casual they may be each ingenuous remark is endowed by the anorexic with a subtle meaning:

'I expect you've read this haven't you?' (She hasn't but assumes that she ought to have done.)

'I don't think we've got it in your size.' (The girl can see she's monstrous.)

'I don't suppose you're worried about revision for finals.' (No one takes *her* academic prospects seriously.)

The only way to avoid the pain of these encounters is to avoid the encounters themselves. As long as anorexic thinking persists no amount of rational persuasion will convince a person who is dominated by it that her interpretation of what she hears is distorted. The anorexic becomes increasingly unsociable and restricts her contacts with other people to an irreducible minimum.

She cannot escape entirely from the attention of those who already know her well and those who live with her, the family or her flatmates, but her attitudes to them will change. Those who knew her well before the onset of anorexic thinking may have no difficulty in observing that her uncharacteristic behaviour is often a charade, designed to dissemble rather than to clarify, but they cannot interpret the meaning of what is concealed. Parents of anorexics will say 'She's just not like herself any more, she's changed so much,' implying that they are aware of the false 'front' but still unaware of its function.

These comments are made with sadness or bewilderment but they can be music in the ears of the anorexic. Like other worried statements about her weight or appearance they confirm her sense of mastery over her grosser self and provide another of the infrequent but welcome occasions when, unworthy as she is, she experiences a paradoxical sense of superiority over those who are less disciplined.

These rare moments of elation which, by sustaining the anorexic's zeal constitute a real danger in themselves, are always followed by a decline into fear and anxiety which has been increased rather than diminished by the brief moment of euphoria.

The anorexic 'highs', which result from registering a satisfactory (lower) weight or from a particularly ingenious method of food disposal, tend to become increasingly less rewarding and shorter in duration. Virginia, whose description of communication between anorexic patients and hospital staff was quoted in Chapter 5, illustrates for us this swing from high to low in the following short poem:

On Being 'High'

My own identity flooding on me.
Hard days by high above all people
in the clouds, superior, apart, splitting apart,
then frightened, alone, hunger for people too.
Sundays, long sunny afternoons
panic at the sun
shining long, endless trapped Sundays
lurched into emptiness
Hard biting winds cold, cold, running
running reckless, lost in the rain
round cities made for cars
wetter and wetter
running from hell and to hell.

In the letter to the *Guardian* quoted in Chapter 5, the correspondent said that, in her opinion, insufficient emphasis was placed on the horror and misery of the eating sickness by those who write about it. As an expression of a personal view the statement may well have been valid for the writer who based it on her own experience of the illness many years previously. But it would be factually inaccurate as well as unnecessarily discouraging to suggest that all the unhappy possibilities associated with it which we have described in this book will inevitably occur in each and every case of anorexia nervosa. And although the fundamental and typical anorexic feelings will be common to all anorexics, their duration and intensity will vary from person to person. It follows therefore that some will get better more quickly than others and stay well while some may relapse after a period of improvement.

Although there is much which still needs to be learned about the reasons for these variations and for the diversity of behaviour which can occur, one factor is constant; there can be no diagnosis of anorexia nervosa without it and while it does persist no real recovery is possible. We refer of course to anorexic thinking, and to the vital necessity of helping the sufferer to change it which is crucial to the successful outcome of treatment.

The recognition that anorexia nervosa is about the feelings which are responsible for the self-destructive attitudes which spring from them leads to the natural assumption that the psychiatrist should be the person to put matters right for the sufferer. Once overall physical safety has been assured the work needed to overcome the illness must take place within the patient's mind where the original idea was conceived and developed into the philosophy of anorexic life.

Psychiatry as the appropriate source of help seems a reasonable assumption which has probably justified the hopes of anorexics and their families more often than it has disappointed them. But there is not, and there may never be, a reservoir of readily available psychiatric help sufficient to meet potential need. In Britain, and possibly in other countries where anorexia nervosa is equally prevalent, it is necessary to seek for the specialist in the treatment of the disorder sometimes from city to city or from rural area to a comparatively distant town.

Those who are known to have this special interest receive requests for advice from all over the country from sufferers, their families, their friends and people who are professionally concerned with their care. Most of these are aware that effective therapeutic help cannot be supplied from a distance but must be sought close at hand. Many, however, express their own need to understand the philosophy of the anorexic life style and the ideas from which it springs. This need is sometimes expressed as a plea for an accurate assessment of the precise cause of the particular eating sickness to which the subject of their enquiry has succumbed. They imply that if such an assessment, should it be made, confirms their own hypothesis, this will relieve their anxiety and justify their request for advice.

Even if such assessment were possible in the absence of direct personal contact with the subject it would still leave unanswered the question of what kind of help would be most useful and acceptable to those concerned. Every family, every relationship is different. It is not possible to define a standard procedure which any relative of an anorexic may adopt and use in the confident hope of a standard result. When offering guidance to would-be therapists it is easier for those with experience to be emphatic about what *not* to do than to state categorically what another therapist *must* do. The recovery of many anorexics has been initiated by their response to an instinctive action or an intuitive comment from someone they once trusted and had newly begun to trust again. Others have related how the consistent repetition of certain simple rational statements eventually convinced them of the irrationality of their own anorexic view.

In each case trust was the critical factor. No one can be persuaded to change their mind by someone they mistrust. This is as true for others who care about the anorexic as it is for the therapist. Everyone who knows her wants their day-to-day relationship with the anorexic to contribute to her recovery rather than to hinder it. When the anorexic's negative reactions make them fear they are doing more harm than good they wonder what they are doing 'wrong' and question whether it might be in the anorexic's best interest to spend some time in the care of those less emotionally involved.

There is no dogmatic answer to these questions but when the

'scrambled' messages which are passing between the anorexic and her family are causing increasing unhappiness to all of them it is imperative to ease this situation. One way or another, according to the resources available, some clarification is needed which will result in clear communication being established. The extent to which this can be used positively varies, but for many families the resulting openness comes as a relief and a revelation. Anxiety diminishes and a new intimacy develops between members of the family within which the anorexic can mature in her own way without fear of infringing the constraints which she had imposed on herself in the belief that they derived from the ethos of the family.

Whether the anorexic's previous perception of this ethos was in fact accurate or not it may subsequently undergo some modification anyway in the light of her more realistic view of the world. But this is only likely to happen when the purpose of the family's discourse together is the sharing of ideas and feelings without the overriding need to avoid upsetting each other which has hitherto inhibited their spontaneity and contributed to the confusion of their aims. It is, therefore, important to find ways of helping anorexics and their families to allow communication between them to fulfil its true purpose. People need to be able to say what they really mean and to express their own feelings without anticipating the kind of traumatic response so painful for any family which experiences overwhelming tides of emotion as a threat to its own stability.

When a family no longer fears this threat the emotional eruptions which are an inevitable feature of family life can be tolerated and recognised as signs of development and growth rather than of disintegration and change for the worse.

The family of an anorexic who has not been living at home with her parents during the greater part of her illness may be less immediately involved in this process of adjustment. To the anorexic who is only beginning to learn to trust her own instincts in such matters the closer involvement of her family, after she has already begun to separate from them, may not seem like a positive step in the right direction. But the separated anorexic has nevertheless to make the same adjustments to emotional independence from her family as the younger girl who is still, in practical terms, a child at home. The separated girl has to do the work inside her head and much of the time alone. But although one of them is physically distant from her parents the rethinking that each must do is similar in many ways.

For the family the difference may lie in the stage of maturity at which the anorexic was 'frozen' when anorexic thinking took over. Although during the illness she may have kept up academically she will almost certainly have fallen behind in terms of emotional maturation.

As she gradually resumes her interest in a fuller social and emotional life she will have some lost ground to recover to catch up with her chronological age. We know from experience how swiftly, once it has started, this catching up can take place, particularly when the encouragement of family and friends is offered in a way which the anorexic can readily accept.

Such encouragement needs to be aimed at confirming that the anorexic's increasing confidence in her own autonomy is welcomed by those who care for her. She needs to know that she can safely reduce her dependence on them without arousing their anxiety or appearing ungrateful. Separation should not be seen, by her or by her family, as loss but as a movement from the status of child into that of adulthood and the new relationships which will naturally follow.

The more fully everyone concerned understands what must happen the easier these changes will be. This is true for the whole process of the illness and its complexities as we have indicated throughout this book. Although we have stated what we believe to be the principles which should govern the successful treatment of anorexia nervosa, we have offered recommendations rather than instructions on how these principles should be implemented in order to effect a lasting cure. And though it is also possible to categorise certain strategems which seem to be helpful in specific instances, the localised improvement which has often followed their use is not a cure of the illness. Nor can the teaching of such strategems be a substitute for the re-education process which is essential to achieve a complete and permanent change in the anorexic's philosophy and life style.

In the next chapter we will describe some of the feelings which arise in those concerned during recovery.

8 Recovery

It seemed as though the whole thing got set in concrete . . .' *A father's*
description of a stage in his daughter's anorexic illness

The comparison with rock-hard concrete seems a particularly apt
simile to describe not only the way in which anorexic illness can
crystallise but also the impression of immutability and inertia
which is conveyed to those who care about the sufferer.

Parents, relatives and therapists confronted by what they
experience as intransigence may feel quite powerless. The only
change which, at that stage, appears at all possible is a change for
the worse. Often it appears to be the only one which the sufferer
either envisages or desires. In these circumstances it is understandable that the fears and anxieties of those most closely
involved will increase to a level which threatens the emotional
equilibrium of the whole group. Both the anxieties of the
therapist and the fears of the relatives may be expressed in a way
which is interpreted by the anorexic as anger or aggression
towards herself. If, instead of being expressed directly to the
sufferer, these anxieties are displaced, the resulting disturbances
in other relationships within the family will provide the
anorexic with further opportunities for self-reproach.

The anorexic's acceptance of responsibility for this dis-
turbance is unlikely to be challenged; it may even be tacitly or
explicitly confirmed. The familiar exhortation to consider how
much worry the sufferer is causing mother, father and others is
usually superfluous since acute awareness of this is already an
integral part of the whole miserable experience.

Any situation in which anxiety is the predominating feature is always a potentially dangerous one, however that anxiety is dealt with. In the case of anorexia nervosa the words and actions precipitated by feelings of fear and anxiety are more likely to accelerate than to reverse the crystallising process of the illness.

The therapeutic task at this stage is, therefore, a challenging one. It is not surprising that many therapists, already daunted by the diagnostic label of anorexia nervosa, are often further discouraged by the apparent failure of their initial attempts at treatment. 'Plough thou the rock until it bear . . . Learn from fears to vanquish fears, to hope, for thou dar'st not despair.' The words of the poet Francis Thompson are apt but not comforting and indeed the consequences of succumbing to despair may be tragic for both the anorexic and those caring for her. Fortunately the experience of such emotional extremes is not an inevitable accompaniment of treatment for everyone with an eating sickness. We know there are some people with such problems whose illness does not crystallise and who resume normal eating patterns without medical intervention; but we also know of people who have not recovered but have remained inside their anorexic fortress inaccessible to any kind of healing intervention medical or otherwise. Some of these have died.

When anorexia nervosa has become 'set in concrete' the sufferer is also immobilised and quite unable to take even the first tentative step towards recovery without intervention and assistance from an outside source. This imposes a serious responsibility on those whose experience has made them acutely aware of the dangers of non-intervention or postponement in the forlorn hope of a spontaneous recovery. The modern therapist, faced with a dangerously crystallised case of anorexia nervosa, has his or her own internal conflict to resolve. It is likely that the therapist came to maturity learning his or her treatment skills within one of the enlightened schools which teaches that success in therapy is only possible if the patient wills it consciously or unconsciously and that this must be established before treatment can start. If this principle were rigidly applied by every therapist confronted by a starving anorexic the mortality figures would be higher than those which are currently published.

On the other hand if a therapist believes that one death from anorexia nervosa is one too many, and in addition believes that it may be avoidable, the resolution of any conflict between therapeutic principles and the imperative needs of the situation becomes possible. Such resolution will, however, always be painful and this is perhaps why many therapists consider it wiser not to combine the treatment of people suffering from anorexia nervosa with that of patients with widely differing problems which require a quite different approach. The treatment of anorexia nervosa requires that therapists remain constant while tolerating both the crises and the tedium of the illness.

The first step, therefore, on the road to recovery for the anorexic is to locate someone who is willing to help despite the inevitable difficulties inherent in the task, someone who can inspire the necessary confidence in the sufferer to start what may be a long arduous journey.

We have already seen in Chapter 3 how, even when the parents of Laura Scott had decided to seek help as quickly as possible, there was still an inevitable delay of several weeks before they obtained their first clinic appointment. It is not unusual for this period to be even longer. The anorexic herself may succeed in temporising, clinics may be fully booked or staff may be away. Events can conspire in various ways to extend this waiting period until by the time the patient, as she has then become, reaches the clinic she is in a critical condition requiring a crucial decision on the immediate course of action. This is what happened to Laura Scott. The crystallisation process which was already beginning had been accelerated during the waiting time possibly in response to the initial efforts of her family and her doctor to challenge her anorexic behaviour. This acceleration was quite evident to her parents who were becoming increasingly sensitive to all the manifestations of the illness. They were already beginning to question the wisdom of their decision to seek psychiatric help while, at the same time, they wanted desperately to be reassured that they had done the right thing. The only convincing proof of this which could have brought them comfort would have been an immediate positive response by Laura to initiation of treatment followed by a speedy cure. Nothing in the dynamics of the situation made such an easy solution probable though such hopes in any parents of an anorexic child are wholly understandable. In families like the Scotts which are unused to failure the slow pace of recovery from anorexia nervosa can made excessive demands on their tolerance and patience.

When Laura and her parents arrived at the clinic it was Mrs Scott who appeared to be the natural leader, the protagonist, the one on whom responsibility had devolved. Mr Scott, despite his powerful physical presence, and the bearing and manner of a man accustomed to succeed in his enterprises, seemed almost diffident and reluctant to be involved in the consultation process. Although the arrangements for the meeting had specifically included both parents, Mr Scott initially suggested that he should drop Laura and his wife at the clinic, make a business call in town, and return later to hear the consultant's opinion. He seemed surprised at the degree of importance which the clinic staff accorded to his presence and even more so when he was asked to participate in and contribute to the preliminary discussions.

Seated together in the busy reception area during the uneasy waiting period between their early arrival and the appointment time the Scotts looked unhappy and vulnerable. Laura, pale and tense despite her effort to maintain an air of resigned composure, followed every movement of the clinic staff; her large and beautiful eyes carefully avoiding contact with all the other eyes whose gaze was drawn by her grotesque emaciation. Her parents, aware of this reaction to Laura's appearance, experienced once again the painful feeling to which they were daily becoming more accustomed. The silent appraisal by strangers made them regret their inability to arrange private help or a purely medical consultation. They felt as though they were defendants awaiting the hearing of a case against them in which they were unlikely to be fairly or fully represented.

The psychiatrist, when she came to find them, explained that while she talked with Laura one of her colleagues would talk to Mr and Mrs Scott. After this they would all meet again with the consultant for a discussion about how best to implement whatever plan had been agreed. The plan and its implementation would be based on the consultant's recommendation after he had heard the full history of Laura's eating disorder.

The Scotts were uncertain whether this approach was reassuring or the reverse. It was certainly unexpected and Mr Scott would have preferred a less tentative one which stressed the responsibility and competence of the health authority to offer a service rather than the patient and family's obligation to share the task. His wife however seemed glad of the chance to give and to receive information which she felt was relevant.

When the co-worker (in this case a psychiatric social worker) explained to the Scotts that what happened next would depend largely on what was taking place at that moment between Laura and the psychiatrist in the room along the corridor, they both looked dismayed. Did the psychiatrist realise that Laura, once the soul of rectitude with such shining integrity that she had seemed almost set apart from her contemporaries, was now a stranger to truth? Mrs Scott was relieved by assurances that such changes were characteristic of anorexia nervosa but Mr Scott was further discouraged. The tension between them was evident and both agreed that it seemed to increase in direct proportion to Laura's weight loss, it affected not only their relations with each other but also with the rest of the family. This was distressing to both parents; it underlined for Mr Scott the urgency of the situation and the importance of preventing Laura's condition from causing further disruption in the life of the family.

Mrs Scott was clearly as convinced as her husband of the imperative need for action of some kind but she seemed to be in two minds as to what kind of action was either desirable or possible. She felt there could be no approach which they had not already tried, without effect, except perhaps a physically coercive one and it distressed her even to mention the possibility of such measures.

It seemed then natural and appropriate for the social worker to ask, as she usually did at these first meetings, whether the Scotts would like to know about the way in which Laura's difficulties would be examined and how a decision about possible courses of action could be made. It would be useful to relate this information to their own expectations.

The Scotts seemed faintly surprised. Their expectations, as far as Mr Scott was concerned, were straightforward. Surely, he implied, the consultant with his reputed expertise in the treatment of this particular problem would in due course give an opinion. Whatever he said they had already decided to accept wholeheartedly. They would go along with whatever he recommended; there was little point in seeking advice unless one was prepared to accept it. They were also more than willing to do anything they could to ensure that the psychiatrist was made aware of the full extent of Laura's illness. Their chief anxiety was that such relevant information might not be conveyed by Laura herself. Each had a mental picture of their daughter, sitting in the psychiatrist's room, mute and tearful, uttering no words at all or alternatively responding to questions brightly and fluently with a shallow stream of meaningless rationalisations which bore no relation to the reality of her predicament. They were not sure which was the more likely nor which could be the most damaging to their hopes for immediate and successful treatment. They therefore welcomed the opportunity to supply the necessary factual information themselves and Mr Scott's accuracy and precision with regard to dates and the chronology of Laura's life contrasted with his wife's tendency to relate individual events to the background history of the family. Time sequence for her was conveyed by phrases such as 'After your mother died', 'In our old house', or 'After we moved', using these events as 'markers' in a way that made Mr Scott apologise good naturedly for her digressions.

Mr Scott's factual accuracy combined with his wife's illuminating perspective provided a valuable structural background to the history of Laura's illness. His objectivity made him seem less emotionally vulnerable than Mrs Scott whose narrative style was so defenceless it seemed almost apologetic. She was sometimes willing to assume responsibility for events which subsequently, within the context of the family, had been judged to be ill-advised. The timing of her pregnancies was a significant example of this tendency although it was evident that the birth of all their children had been a major source of satisfaction to both parents and had provided the mainspring of their lives. It was the strength of their commitment to the interests of their children which made Laura's illness so painful and bewildering for them.

Throughout the time during which parents and social worker were concentrating on the effort to communicate with each other, striving for accuracy and for the clearest way to express their thoughts, each had a silent preoccupation. What was happening in the room where Laura and the psychiatrist were supposed to be similarly occupied? What would happen next? Mr Scott glanced at his watch. Over an hour had passed. The social worker, seeing the gesture, suggested a respite while she went to investigate.

In the psychiatrist's room Laura in a low chair, her legs like two blue denim covered sticks sharply angled at the knee, clutched a rolled up handkerchief in her red and blue claw-like hands. She had a little hectic flush near each protrusive cheekbone. The psychiatrist, similarly flushed, looked serious but less distressed. She said that Laura had begun to discuss her problem and they had established a basis for further discussion but first they must all share their information with each other and with the consultant.

Laura rejoined her parents in the waiting area while psychiatrist and co-worker talked with the consultant.

Laura's weight was 68% of what would be healthy and reasonable for her age and height. It was in the grey area around the borderline between maximum danger and high risk, between the urgent need for hospital admission and the possibility of effective out-patient care. The decision as to which to recommend depended on two things. First the pattern of weight loss, was it static at this point or still falling? How quickly had it dropped so low? The only clearly recorded figure was the locum family doctor's which was several pounds higher and as many weeks earlier. Laura was losing at least a pound a week. This could not be allowed to continue unchecked but at 68 per cent there was just enough room to manoeuvre. Out-patient care might be possible if everyone involved was prepared to help to make it effective. The second consideration was how much could Laura herself and her family do to avoid the necessity of admission to hospital? It was assumed that the Scotts would prefer any arrangement or suggestion other than treatment in a psychiatric hospital.

This assumption was entirely correct as far as Laura was concerned, partially so for Mrs Scott, who had some reservations, but Mr Scott expressed strong misgivings. He was sure further delay would be a mistake and wanted positive action as soon as possible; for him hospitalisation would indicate acceptance of responsibility for Laura's wellbeing by those who were apparently qualified to treat her particular malady. He knew the family would be unable to alter Laura's eating habits and, since they must be altered to save her life, there was no alternative. He understood Laura's aversion to hospital which was why he believed that treatment in a medical ward would be a less unhappy experience, for the family as well as for Laura, than her admission to a psychiatric unit.

When Laura and her parents went together to talk to the consultant the room seemed full of people. There were two medical students as well as the psychiatrist and the social worker. Mr and Mrs Scott had responded to the standard enquiry regarding their willingness to accept the presence of students by deferring to Laura who, with downcast eyes and a tiny sideways movement of her head, accompanied by a shrug of one shoulder, seemed to imply consent. When they were all seated and beginning to discuss plans for her welfare she was overwhelmed, diminished by her incredible frailty which contrasted strongly with the robust appearance of the young students.

During the ensuing discussion Laura's short, whispered comments and responses had to be amplified and interpreted by the psychiatrist who gave an outline of what she had attempted to negotiate with Laura during their hour-long interview.

The diagnosis of anorexia nervosa had been established and was agreed by everyone, except Laura; so was the necessity of helping her to recover from it. The task which faced them all was to decide what part each of them could play in order to achieve that goal.

The consultant explained his view of the situation and what options were available to the treatment team. He also explained how important it was to know the extent to which Laura might be able to co-operate with a plan based on out-patient care supplemented by help for her, and for her family, through regular meetings in the clinic or at home if at any time that should seem appropriate.

Despite the unhurried patience with which their enquiries were pursued Laura was unable to talk to the consultant and his team in the way she had done earlier with the psychiatrist alone. Full participation in such a public discussion, even had she not been the subject of it, would have presented a daunting challenge. She was the youngest person present, surrounded by a roomful of strangers dominated by the consultant who was wearing a suit closely resembling her father's board-room outfit. Her parents seemed to be allied with this alien group and the two students with whom she might have been able to identify since they were her older sister's generation were similarly distant and remote. She was aware of their eyes fixed alternately on her and on the consultant when he spoke and though she avoided looking directly at them she was struck by the studious blankness of their faces as though such impassivity was a condition of their attendance. It was not only the composition of the group which made Laura feel unequal to responding adequately to their demands; she was tired and dispirited. She had just endured an hour-long interview which had signalled for her the end of her hopes of maintaining the secret life which for months past had been her only inspiration.

The realisation by Laura that her private world was about to be invaded, by forces which were being marshalled to breach her defences filled her with terror. Her thoughts were in turmoil and at that moment she wanted, more than anything, to get away from these people so that she could plan her resistance to their assault upon her. This had to be done alone; she had no ally, totally committed to her cause, who could be trusted not to undermine and betray her.

She also needed time to reflect on her interview with the psychiatrist and to decide whether she dared to accept the risk of another one. The suggestion of further meetings was the dominating impression which Laura retained from their encounter and her feelings on the matter were mixed. Her initial defensiveness, which had become an automatic response, had not evoked in the psychiatrist the same reactions which had become so familiar in other people during the past weeks. Nor had she, as she had anticipated, been persistently questioned about her motives for her dietary regime. She was less anxious than she had expected to be about the outcome of the consultation.

The proposal which the consultant now outlined to Laura's parents was that they should all meet again at the same time two weeks later. Meanwhile the aim would be to help Laura to fulfil the undertaking she had given not to lose any more weight during that time. This surprised Mr Scott to whom, having spent most of the morning sharing all their deliberations, it came as an anti-climax. He was persuaded by the doctors, and by his wife who welcomed the proposal, that if Laura could maintain the same weight for two weeks thus halting the present downward drift it would be a positive step; but if the downward trend could not be halted hospital admission might then be considered.

Although Laura had insisted that she was in full control of her eating and her weight and that no power on earth would make her go into hospital the psychiatrist had suggested that the task of holding a steady weight might prove too difficult. This had been expressed as a warning rather than a threat and offered in tones intended to reassure Laura that failure should not be regarded as disaster. Laura accepted the psychiatrist's prediction in silence feeling it was unnecessary to point out that from her own point of view the only likely disaster would be weight gain and this she was confident could be avoided. She had a feeling of being drawn into some kind of negotiation rather than being faced with an ultimatum. She experienced a mixture of relief and apprehension.

The psychiatrist then gave the Scotts some practical advice on how to help Laura to sustain her present level of food intake without increasing the already high anxiety level of all concerned. During this final stage of the consultation, which was more relaxed and informal than the earlier part, there was a lessening of tension and the Scotts were able to put questions, to make comments and to receive answers which though not as good as they had hoped were at least better than they had feared.

The family left the clinic with a mixture of feelings. Laura's equilibrium had been disturbed; she realised that the talk with the psychiatrist had been the 'beginning of the end' but she was not sure what it would be the end *of* nor whether what came afterwards would be better or worse. It had certainly been a turning point of some sort and she decided that she would keep the next appointment if only to demonstrate to the doctors, and prove to herself yet again, the effectiveness of her control. Mr and Mrs Scott felt both relief and disappointment at the outcome of the visit. They had expected more, by which they agreed when they discussed it together later, they probably meant 'worse' for Laura rather than for themselves. Their personal reaction to this their first encounter with psychiatry was a sense of having been remanded pending further investigations.

Dismay was Laura's initial reaction when, two weeks later, the psychiatrist weighed her and recorded a figure lower than the previous one by the smallest amount which the clinic scales could accurately convey, about half a pound or a little less. An equivalent gain would, admittedly, have been unbearable but she feared this small loss might provoke some fearful retribution and was, therefore, uneasy.

The psychiatrist was non-committal and was more interested to hear from Laura what she felt and had been feeling during the past two weeks than to pronounce definitely on the weight loss. She then pointed out that what had happened was the expected result of the difficulties about which she had tried to warn Laura at their first meeting. Laura, who had previously discounted these warnings, found it easier this time to talk about her feelings and to continue for the next hour a discussion which became the first of many to take place over a period of months. By mutual, tacit consent, treatment had begun.

After the second appointment Laura's parents ceased to accompany her to the clinic regularly but there were occasions during the ensuing months when at their own request or in response to a suggestion by the psychiatrist they went together or individually to talk about specific features of the process of recovery on which Laura had embarked and to which, despite several setbacks, she remained committed until its satisfactory conclusion.

Mr and Mrs Scott gradually became acquainted with the psychiatrist but they never became familiar with her, nor she with them since their perceptions of each other were derived for the most part from a vicarious relationship based on the communication link provided by Laura. They did form a more direct relationship in their own right with the social worker. This was neither as personally significant nor as long lasting as that which developed between Laura and her therapist but it served to comfort them and by doing so encouraged their efforts to help Laura through the difficulties which arose during the arduous recovery period.

Her parents' ability and willingness to express their pessimistic and negative feelings about Laura's illness provided insights into the possible precipitants of it. In due course the progressive transformation of their feelings into more positive and optimistic ones similarly confirmed the changes that were taking place in Laura's anorexic thinking and behaviour.

Despite the urgency surrounding the first referral to the clinic, and the equivocal result of deferring for two weeks the decision about the best form of treatment, Laura never did go into hospital although it was discussed during one crisis period. She duly sat her advanced level examinations but the results, adequate enough in that she obtained passes in all of them, were a disappointment. Believing that she was expected to achieve the highest grades she only managed what she regarded as little better than failure by being placed somewhat lower than this. She thought she had let everyone down. By that time, however, she had been working long enough with her therapist to have begun to learn how to cope with such realities. It was the first of many similar challenges. Some of these she took in her stride but others were experienced as setbacks. With the help of her therapist she learned to turn the setbacks into training exercises by recognising that each time she overcame one she emerged a little stronger than she had been before. Thus slowly and erratically her confidence – and her weight – grew to levels, which were both appropriate and acceptable until as a happy and healthy second-year undergraduate she was finally discharged.

The difficulties intrinsic to recovery from anorexia nervosa have already been mentioned in Chapter 3 and in Chapter 5 where reference was also made to the need to recognise that sufferers, their families and their therapists, will have to tolerate a rate of progress slower than any of them would wish. The fact that these particular difficulties can arise when things are ostensibly improving suggests that they may be the expression of the pain and discomfort inherent in all adaptation to change and growth even when that change is inevitable and even desirable. When such desired change comes unbearably slowly or comes, at long last, in forms which were not anticipated the discomfort of those who await it is increased.

Some of the things which anorexics may say and do, during the process of trying to change their anorexic ways, distress and even alarm their families and their friends. It is not unusual for parents to declare that their daughter is 'getting worse' even if there has been weight gain and some modification of anorexic behaviour. This apparent paradox also makes the other difficulties harder to understand. Even the anorexic herself does not always know what is happening to her but at least, if she is lucky, she has a therapist who does. The family may have no one and no previous experience on which to rely for inspiration and support.

It can be bewildering when the first welcome sign of a slight weight gain does not produce in the anorexic the same response as it does in everyone else. Relief, satisfaction and hopes of further and greater gains are all expressed cheerfully in phrases such as 'It's marvellous to see you looking so much better' or 'You'll soon be your old self again.' However carefully the speakers choose their words to avoid the dreaded implications of any personal comment the anorexic can rarely respond with enthusiasm to such encouragement. Even if she has won the first round of the fight against anorexic thinking there will be a hard contest before the final victory. The fear of loss of control leading to gross and disastrous overweight is still strong and remarks about her initial gains, even from her nearest and dearest, only reinforce the fear. 'I love my family but I can't get fat for them,' wrote one anorexic girl speaking for countless others who have felt the same.

Even if they are too small to satisfy anyone else concerned the anorexic's first weight gains will require from her some relaxation of that iron control which has become the principal ruling force of her inner life. Whatever this frightening act of abdication signifies to anyone else the anorexic will experience it as capitulation unless the therapist can persuade her that it is safe to allow herself such latitude. The resulting liberation, if it is successful, may then be extended to include those other aspects of the sufferer's life which have also become subordinate to the iron rule. She may dare to allow herself the luxury of expressing raw emotion without first processing it through her internal refinery to eliminate the 'coarse' elements of instinctive feeling leaving only the purer one of what is expected and therefore right.

The release of emotions, hitherto so carefully distilled that their existence had hardly been suspected, may result in unaccustomed weeping or outbursts of anger which strain the patience of friends and members of the family. Those who remember the anorexic as she was before the illness often find it hard to recognise such uncharacteristic behaviour as a change for the better. Some parents fearing the loss, perhaps for ever, of the child in whom they had invested so much hope, increasingly extol her previous attributes and character in the manner of those who mourn their beloved dead. Even when the recession of the anorexic illness eventually becomes apparent they may still deplore the cost in wasted years of family life while it was running its interminable course.

Fortunately if the impetus which started the movement of the anorexic towards recovery can be sustained or increased it will carry her through these difficulties; the resolution of them often being followed by the enhancement of relationships between her and her family as well as with others whose friendship she had regarded as unattainable. The expansion of social life resulting from increased confidence will bring its own problems, indeed every forward step towards recovery from anorexia nervosa requires the resolution of another difficulty. It is this which gives the process the familiar 'Two steps forward, one step back' effect. Such erratic progress demands patience from everyone concerned including the therapist on whose constancy and consistency the anorexic will depend for the unlimited encouragement needed to continue the struggle. The first tentative attempts by recovering anorexics to resume an appropriate social life are often seen as disastrous failures in their anorexic view which does not allow recognition of the courage needed to have made the effort in the first place.

The latent periods of plateaux between each achievement or episode can be equally frustrating for all concerned. Although the weight itself has ceased to be the critical factor which it has earlier been, considerable tension may still arise during these seemingly inactive periods, particularly if a slight drop in weight occurs. The imminence of a significant date can increase the tension. This may be a scheduled event in which the participation of the anorexic is expected, a family celebration such as a wedding or anniversary, or it may be something personal to the individual anorexic, a holiday abroad, an interview for a job, a college or a university place. Realistic and possibly painful discussions with the therapist to decide whether her attendance may responsibly be encouraged will take place. Although an important part of getting better is learning to decide for herself what she will do, a girl who has been, or is still, anorexic may need the help of a therapist before she can arrive at a decision. The making of choices with confidence and serenity is not the anorexic's strong point as we have seen in previous chapters. The task becomes even harder once the dissolution of the rigid framework of reference on which the anorexic thinking was based has begun to be replaced by a more flexible structure. The feeling of quite literally not knowing 'what to do for the *best*' and whose interests ought to be given first consideration can amount to panic.

In addition to these internal problems there are other practical ones directly related to food and eating. Since the beginning of recorded history the friendships and social activities of mankind have been sustained and nourished by the sharing of food and drink. Even the briefest social interaction is likely to involve at least a cup of coffee or a coke and if people are to spend any significant amount of time together they will, sooner or later, eat together as well. The condition is as inevitable as the human need of people for each other's company. Equally inevitable is the reaction of those suffering from eating disorders to the hazards and the misery of social occasions involving the consumption of food. After the descriptions in earlier chapters of this book it hardly seems necessary to enlarge on the attitude of sufferers and the reasons for the policy to which they subscribe: 'Eating in company is both agonising and dangerous, eating in company is *out*.'

Learning to regain the ability to eat socially without embarrassment, distress or the need for subsequent vomiting is one of the difficult things to be done before full social integration is achieved. Like the other things which must be learnt it demands patience, perseverance and the ability to accept occasional failures and setbacks as a normal part of life in an imperfect world.

For those whose aspirations are cast in the classic anorexic mould of total perfection and ultimate achievement the gradual acceptance of an essentially realistic 'You can't win 'em all' philosophy is perhaps the central and most crucial task which faces them. Unless they achieve this they will not escape from the tyranny of a need for human perfection which can never in the nature of things be wholly satisfied.

The rediscovery of the ability to laugh as well as to cry is a welcome sign indicating that perfectionist thinking, almost childlike, with its clear-cut black and white, right or wrong and nothing in between characteristics, is beginning to yield to a realistic and more mature view which recognises the extent and complexity of the gradations between opposing poles. This maturity, when it is achieved, enables the anorexic to tolerate her own shortcomings and in addition to acknowledge her own intrinsic worth. By learning to take herself less seriously she comes to value herself more and to accept that not only what she does but also what she is can have value for others. Now when she is complimented on her appearance, her achievements or merely for being herself she can accept the comments at face value and respond accordingly.

This clearer more straightforward communication, without the constant anorexic misinterpretations described in Chapter 5 and Chapter 7 leads to an increasing mutuality in the anorexic's dealings with other people. She begins to notice and to care more about the things they do and what they are thinking and feeling. She becomes interested in the prospect of new friendships and the resumption of old ones. She begins to come alive again.

Sometimes there is a price to be paid for this renewed participation in the life from which the anorexic had apparently withdrawn. The family may find that the effort required to come to terms with some of the aspects of recovery from the illness is almost as great as that needed to tolerate the effect of its symptoms. This may also be true of the anorexic herself. Although she is sometimes surprised and gratified by her successful attempts to do an increasing number of things, for which she had regarded herself as disqualified, the not-yet-fully recovered anorexic may still be disturbed when she allows herself to recognise and acknowledge the strength and the implications of some of her current thoughts and feelings. The task of dealing with the inner turmoil which so often occurs at this stage of recovery leaves the anorexic with no reserves of emotional strength and insight on which to draw. She is unlikely to be able to do much to assist her family with their task of adjustment to and understanding of the processes which are taking place within the anorexic and the behaviour which results from them.

The relationships between the anorexic and the concerned group which in addition to the therapist and the patient's family may also include teachers, employers or others such as counsellors or co-therapists, can be difficult at this stage. The difficulties do not arise from fundamental differences between the long-term aims of the various members of the group. All of them want to see the anorexic well and happy at her 'correct' weight, and eating the right amount to ensure that she remains in that state, but there may not be a consensus of opinion between them all as to how this is to be achieved. The results of this disparity of view will be reflected in the varying attitudes and approaches adopted towards the anorexic by diferent people who are significant in her life. Any or all of these approaches may be at variance with that of her therapist.

We have seen anorexics, bewildered by such difficulties, being drawn back into anorexic thinking to escape the conflict, with distressing results for all concerned. Such setbacks need not occur and can be avoided if they are anticipated and the confusions from which they arise are minimised by clear and undistorted communication between the parties concerned.

How may this clarification or synthesis be achieved? We have explained in Chapter 3 why we believe it is not expedient for the individual who is the personal therapist of an anorexic patient to become deeply involved in the politics of the family. The probability is that such involvement will impede rather than assist the anorexic's progress by introducing into her relationship with the therapist an additional element which will, at best, disturb its equilibrium and at worst may damage it irrevocably. Nevertheless something must be done if significant influences are affecting the anorexic in a negative way during long periods of living experience between relatively short episodes of therapy. The role of a co-worker can therefore be seen to have importance not only as a support or solace for the family but as having an essential function in relation to the primary objective of helping the anorexic to recover.

When a co-worker is available to help the family and, when necessary, others in the concerned group to synchronise their efforts, the therapist is free to concentrate on helping the anorexic to cope with all the upsetting manifestations of recovery. It seems superfluous to add that the closest possible co-ordination between therapist and co-worker is essential but we have experienced the adverse results of impaired communication often enough to convince us that co-operative work requires co-operative planning and discussion. A co-worker is powerless and his or her interventions may even be destructive if the role is not conceived as an integral part of the overall treatment plan. If it is discounted, as being merely ancillary, its effectiveness as a positive contribution to recovery will be of equally small value.

We have talked in this chapter about recovery as though it were almost as painful and fraught with difficulty as anorexia nervosa itself and so for many, if not all, anorexics it can be. The following poem written by Virginia now happily recovered from a severe anorexic illness, illustrates this more feelingly than ordinary words can do:

> And so they made me walk along the edge of the abyss
> And said 'You must conquer your fear of the depths or
>   we shall grieve for ever how you fell'
> But I was weak at the knees and the abyss beckoned me
>   and I did not know what lay at the end of the path
>   anyway
> They said it was a green and pleasant land but I could
>   not believe them as I had not seen it myself and
>   thought they had
> The Fear was so great that I yearned to fall into the
>   comforting abyss
> But I could not let them down and had to conquer my
> fear and spent a long time crouched hesitating while
> they stood in a safe place fearful for my safety
> and beckoning me to go forward.

The writer of this poem did 'go forward' and in spite of many painful experiences she survived with the ability to express her feelings about the events with sensitivity and insight.

Another recovered anorexic with similar ability even suggested, when describing her sense of wellbeing that the illness had been of positive value to her:

In a strange way, though, I owe a lot of this to anorexia. Not only can you appreciate life far more through having so nearly lost it, but somehow through it all – maybe through struggling to prove myself – I have become the person I am. Looking back, I think that always, behind my painfully shy, dull and studious exterior there was a talkative, bouncy extrovert longing to get out! That, I'm sure, was one of the many factors that caused my illness; some of the others I told you about, many I can't even guess at.

From the many anorexics willing to express their feelings with the same facility as those whom we have quoted much can be learnt about the experience of emerging from an anorexic illness. It is only by achieving an understanding of these feelings that therapists are able to offer guidance which is acceptable, and therefore effective, on coping with some of the physical aspects of recovery. Patients and their families often seek such guidance and in the next chapter, in which we shall hear from recovered anorexics what it is like to be well again, we shall describe some of the things which may happen to an undernourished body when normal feeding is resumed.

9 Who Gets Better?

A comprehensive review of all the available statistical information about anorexia nervosa should persuade sufferers that from
a mathematical point of view they are very much more likely to
recover from the illness than not to do so.

Although the figures quoted by different researchers and
investigators vary, according to the type of statistical measures
used, there is among them all a broad consensus which suggests
convincingly that the odds are about four to one in favour of
recovery and that a well-motivated and optimistic anorexic will
win the battle against the illness eventually. For some that
eventuality may take longer to achieve than for others but,
sooner or later, the majority should be able to claim a successful
outcome.

A sad little minority group appears repeatedly in all the
published reports and surveys. These are the people who,
despite the efforts of those who care for them, remain still
trapped in an eating sickness, the symptoms of which certainly
diminish the quality of their lives and may even threaten their
existence. Although, when compared with those who have
recovered and those who are still improving, they form the
smallest group, the fate of those for whom help has proved
ineffective must remain a matter of major concern to everyone
who is aware of their predicament. The very fact that they
invariably do constitute a minority is both a challenge and an
incentive. It ought to be possible, by examining the differences
between them and those for whom the outcome is so much

happier, to discover why so many people can and do recover from anorexia nervosa while some still fail to do so.

It seems imperative to search for explanations of why the help which is effective for many can be ineffective for a few. One way of approaching this task is to try and deepen our understanding of how and why the majority succeeded in overcoming anorexia nervosa in the hope of identifying what may have been missing for those who continue to suffer from it.

In many other illnesses where the standard treatment is universally recognised and predictably successful it can be administered with confidence to a passive patient from whom little more is asked than optimistic co-operation. This is not the case with anorexia nervosa. The fact that the number of sufferers who can be expected to recover generally exceeds those who are less likely to do so cannot be attributed to the passive acceptance by the majority of anorexic patients of a recognised and proven method of specific treatment. There is no standard remedy among the diverse range of alternative procedures to which doctors and therapists may have recourse and the passive anorexic patient is not necessarily the one most likely to recover.

Apparent passivity in an anorexic can be as misleading as some of the other deceptive strategies employed to defend her anorexic integrity: it is much more likely to be passive resistance rather than the ingenuous compliance of the patient who is too physically ill to do anything but accept trustingly whatever the doctors suggest. The latter has every reason to comply – a physically ill patient fears that the treatment might fail; the anorexic fears it will succeed.

Traces of this fear linger and re-emerge intermittently even when things are beginning to improve. Getting better can feel to the anorexic every bit as unpleasant as she always thought it would be. It can even feel like getting worse. Some of the physical effects of refeeding to which we referred at the end of the last chapter, besides being uncomfortable in themselves, can also cause anxiety and distress particularly if they are unexpected. In addition the psychological unfreezing which accompanies physical recovery is always a cause of upset to the patient and her family.

For a girl who comes to value control as *the* supreme virtue it is distressing to find that her own control of moods is, from her point of view, slipping badly and she cannot regain her previous calm. From the helpers' point of view the picture is much more that of the gradual melting of an unnatural and frozen emotional rigidity.

In the early years of our work with anorexics we were helped by a motherly and outspoken Welsh assistant nurse. She had, at that time, special responsibility for overseeing the anorexic patients' meals and their extra Complan drinks. More than one casual visitor to the ward obtained an odd impression of our way of working because he or she arrived at the nurses' office to find this nurse enthusiastically inviting her colleagues to rejoice with her because anorexic Mary or Jane 'has got thoroughly upset and is crying her eyes out'.

The visitors found it difficult to believe we were not gloating over a patient's misery rather than sharing our immense relief that this particular Mary or Jane had at last turned the corner and relaxed her iron control enough to acknowledge, experience and express without restraint a negative emotion. 'She'll start to make real progress now' was how our Welsh nurse summed up such events.

As on other occasions when a patient has at last found courage to express some of the long buried anger and resentments they have felt – possibly by disagreeing with the doctor and saying so in a direct and outspoken manner – the therapist's task is to avoid any move which will stifle or abort the process of emotional expression. Our Welsh nursing colleague was in haste to tell the rest of the staff what was happening in order to prevent any new arrival, who might not understand the importance of these first tears, approaching the anorexic and telling her to stop crying or suggesting that such an open display of emotion distressed the other patients.

Learning to allow oneself the full experience and expression of what one actually feels is a vital part of recovery, but the early stages of such learning are easily discouraged. Loving parents, who – by their own preference for 'calming down' and being 'reasonable' in situations when emotions threaten to spill over – have already provided some of the building blocks for the sufferer's over-valuation of control, may not understand the necessity for accepting, allowing and valuing the first tears, the first irritable outbursts or overt disagreements. It is difficult for parents to recognise these as manifestations of recovery. Unwittingly their preference for cool, unemotional, reasonable discussion can reinforce the child's feeling that tears or taunts, tantrums, depressions or acts of defiance are *wrong* and so the little thawed bit gets rapidly refrozen and *control* is again set up to reign as the supreme value.

The anorexic who cries her tears through unchecked to the bitter end discovers two important things. The first reassurance comes when she finds that her tears are not the overflow of a bottomless pool. On the contrary the supply of tears is finite. When she has shed them all she *cannot* cry any more. This discovery is a realistic counter to her former fear that if she once let go and started to cry she would never be able to stop. Fears of irrevocably 'going to pieces' or going 'mad' haunt many anorexics. The actual experience of surviving a formerly unthinkable bout of prolonged crying can and does profoundly lessen these haunting fears.

The other major discovery is that after the crying is over the sufferer actually feels better, not worse, for having cried. The relaxed exhausted bodily state that follows prolonged sobbing is for many girls one of the first experiences of relief from the tightly strung tension (physical, emotional and moral) that is the continuing state of all anorexics who have not yet started to recover. Those who let themselves cry have risked making a practical experiment to find out whether it is always awful to lose control in any kind of way.

When the predicted worst does not happen the sufferer may take courage and try another experiment. Not all anorexics make their discoveries in such large steps. For some the emotional release comes in thousands of tiny steps which one might call micro-episodes. In either case what is necessary to allay the inevitable anxieties which accompany this slow regaining of the capacity to feel and express the full range of human emotions, is repeated, clear and accurate explanation of what is happening and why it happens together with practical information about how to minimise the physical discomfort as well as how to deal with the anxieties. Such information, for those who can get it, is usually sufficient reassurance.

The resurgence of some of the old feelings coupled with alarm at what seems to be happening to the anorexic's body as it is gradually renourished are not really surprising. The physical effects of refeeding, besides being unpleasant, can confuse the anorexic and sometimes her family as well, because their appearance and disappearance does not synchronise with that of the primary effect of malnutrition to which they are secondary. When the starving body, which has been the most obvious visual evidence of food restriction, is beginning to look nourished once more, there is a time lag while the various ancillary processes, which were part of the body's response to starvation, struggle to reverse their previous adaptive strategies.

Hair which has been thinning can only start to grow again when the deficits which had caused it to fall out have not only been made good but the reserves necessary for continued growth have been established which is usually two or three months *after* weight gain has been established as a steady routine. Brittle nails and dry skin may similarly take time to revert to normal while what the anorexic regards as heroic eating habits are being acquired. Since these secondary effects of malnutrition took some time to develop in the first place it is perfectly natural that they should take an equivalent length of time to diminish. Meanwhile the absence of those signs of returning normality which would be most welcome to the anorexic and the appearance of other quite unwelcome ones can justify the feelings, often shared by her family, that things are indeed worse than they had expected them to be at this stage of the illness. Parents who are not forewarned that getting better means more unhappiness at first have been known to withdraw their child from treatment which was actually succeeding.

Perhaps the most universal and most uncomfortable physical symptom which accompanies re-feeding is the bloated feeling and the distension of the stomach which follows eating. Even after a comparatively modest meal the anorexic feels as though she has consumed a gargantuan feast. The discomfort intensifies her preoccupation with that contentious area which has been dominating her thoughts for so long and where an intolerable expansion now seems to be taking place. There is some justification for this conviction because early weight gains do tend to be central rather than peripheral. Like toddlers, anorexics grow larger livers *before* weight gain is redistributed to the limbs. The stick-like arms and legs, which used to provide visible reassurance that she was not becoming gross, are the last traces of the illness to disappear.

The dismay of someone who has been living for months inside a skeleton when that familiar frame, which has housed her very being, starts to expand erratically from the centre is as understandable as the difficulty caused by all the other adjustments which have to be made at the same time. As usual it is the articulate anorexic who describes most vividly the experiences of recovery; this is Virginia's account:

It was starting eating again that was the worst. Instead of eating slowly to keep back with everyone else I ate very quickly to get it over with and had to get up and do things before I had time to think. I felt completely worthless and useless and there didn't seem any point in existing. I frantically busied myself clearing and helping in some sort of effort to justify my existence I suppose. It's hard to describe the feeling of nakedness. All happenings seemed to impinge much more upon me. I couldn't get away from all the things going on round me and there seemed to be twice as many as before . . . I dreaded people noting that I had put on weight. Such harmless phrases as 'You're looking well' or 'You look blooming' would cast me into the depths of despair for the day . . . When I got my periods back I wasn't half as angry as I thought I would be. I had to say to myself 'Look you're not anorexic any more so there's no excuse for any more silly behaviour' and there was relief that they had come back at a weight which I felt was liveable with, but still the most joyful moments of my existence are when I meet an old friend who exclaims on my thinness. I'm on top of the world and I keep a store of these little remarks in my head for the bad times . . . There is a corner of my mind that says 'If only I was under seven stone again' or 'Please God make it all go away and let me be thin again.' . . . I've never seen so many thin people in my life as when I was putting on weight. A short visit to the shops could leave me haunted and miserable ... My only consolation is standing looking at the back of my elbow in a mirror but even that is returning to normal size.

The feelings and reactions described here occur when there is general agreement that the outlook for the anorexic is becoming more hopeful, which is a compelling reason for ensuring that help is available at this critical time. If it should not be and the anorexic's feelings are predominantly painful ones, while everyone else is experiencing an optimism which they expect her to share, she will again be alienated from them. The old sensation of being 'set apart' from others, of living by a different set of rules and criteria, can return all too easily. Many anorexics have succumbed to it again even after giving every sign of recovering physically.

Such relapses demonstrate clearly that quantitative measurements alone – facts and figures relating to weight and calories – are unreliable indicators of progress unless they are supported by a qualitative assessment of the extent of change in the strength and direction of anorexic thought. This has already been said in previous chapters and in relation to different stages of the illness but it is equally important in the present context where we are dealing with the questions of who succeeds in getting better from anorexia nervosa.

Professor Cyril Joad, a regular member of the BBC's *Brains Trust* panel in the early 1940's, invariably responded to every enquiry by saying, 'It depends what you mean by —' inserting the keyword of the original question. The repetition of this catchphrase by a generation of regular listeners popularised not only the professor's method of temporising but more significantly his insistence on grasping not simply the precise definition of the question's keyword but also the questioner's own interpretation of its meaning before attempting to reply.

The question 'What do you mean by recovery from anorexia nervosa?' might evoke a variety of answers. Although there may be general consensus between all those caring for anorexics, nevertheless an individual who has had the illness may have some reservations. If asked the question she is likely to qualify her responses and, paradoxically, it will be the ability to do so, to recognise and accept degrees and variations instead of polar extremes, which will indicate the extent of recovery.

The criteria we use for declaring that a recovery has been achieved are fivefold.

They include the ability to eat three regular meals a day as an ordinary state of affairs while still being able to skip the occasional lunch if pressures at work demand it 'just this once' or, on the other hand, being able to eat without guilt a second unplanned supper on the way home from the cinema if the fish and chips smell good that night.

Weight has to be stable within 15 per cent (more often 10 per cent) of average expected weight without significant fluctuations or excessive worry.

Periods need to have returned and be as regular as they were before the anorexia nervosa started (or alternatively only disappear again because a desired pregnancy has been achieved).

The recovered patient is free to work at a job, occupation or course of study appropriate to her interests and ability and finds that difficulties do not make her withdraw feeling she is the wrong person for the job but, on the contrary, make her involve herself more closely in order to tackle and solve the difficulty.

The final mark of recovery, which is more difficult to assess without knowing the patient's circumstances very intimately, is an age-appropriate degree of emancipation from her family of origin and evidence that she can make new acquaintances, promote some of these acquaintances into friends and develop an age-appropriate close relationship with at least one of these friends.

In passing, it is worth noting that people trapped in chronic anorexia nervosa work very hard at maintaining the circle of friends they had when the illness began. But the ordinary changes of life move these friends on into marriage and parenthood and new jobs on the other side of the country, so that the anorexic, trapped in the unvarying prison of her illness, becomes increasingly lonely as the number of her available friends dwindles away. The one step the sufferer cannot take is to make a *new* friend because this involves self-disclosure; and while the illness reigns the anorexic is dedicated to hiding what she really thinks and feels.

Many anorexics, regarded by all who know them as completely well again, will say that they feel anorexia nervosa has changed them permanently. The majority do not say this with regret. Most even welcome the changes though they admit that they would have preferred to have made them less painfully and the recognition that they and others have suffered during the process makes them reluctant to over-emphasise the finality and completeness of recovery. It is, however, not at all rare for anorexics to say after they are well that they would not have developed as much as they have done in terms of confidence without going through the anorexic illness. The more severe the illness has been the longer it will take for the feelings of sadness to disperse in its aftermath and to be replaced by robust optimism.

This caution seems reasonable rather than unduly pessimistic. No major life event which engages all the faculties of mind and body leaves us totally unaltered. No one, after a severe illness, is exactly the same as they were before and even benign occurrences such as successful participation in highly competitive sporting or other events will take their toll of physical and psychic energy. Having a baby and becoming a parent leads to irrevocable change. Any of these happenings, which are commonplace in general terms but significant in particular, may be accompanied by considerable trauma for the individual concerned in whom the memory of it may persist for a long time before finally being extinguished. It is not surprising that the same thing happens after anorexia nervosa. There seems to be no reason why the effects of an illness so pervasive should be completely eradicated in less time than it took for them to develop and the anorexic who is much better than she was, but not yet as well as she hopes to be, should not cause undue concern.

There is equally no reason why, at this stage of almost but not complete recovery, she should not proceed with whatever plans she has for living and working. She will need to exercise all her newly acquired ability to compromise and to be less exacting and more accepting of herself. She must even begin to like and take care of the body from which she has for so long withheld all comfort. The rigour with which she denied its vital nourishment should be replaced by an equally assiduous attention to the provision of regular and balanced meals. This will be the hard part and the difficulty lies not so much in accepting the discipline of three meals a day, and ensuring that the balance is right, but in feeling free to look forward to and enjoying the consumption of favourite foods without guilt. Indeed the guilt is often the last bit of anorexic thinking to disappear, which may account for the enthusiasm with which the recovering anorexic tackles the question of work, whether academic study or paid employment.

There is rarely, if ever, any need to prompt a recovering anorexic to work. The anxiety of those who care for her is likely to be that she may hope to achieve too much too soon. It is not uncommon for the first job at this stage to be a mistaken choice. There is great value in a deliberate choice of an interim temporary job which is less than the sufferer can do at her best but as much as she can bear to cope with at bad times, for example when depressed or eating erratically. The anorexic then has the chance to learn, with the help of her therapist if she has one, the unwritten but universally recognised rule that everybody is allowed at least one false start. She learns to do 'good enough' work instead of always only her best. As a bona fide member of the 'ordinary' adult world and no longer an outsider she is no exception in this or in any of the other things she begins to experience with new vividness. She is free to give herself the same latitude as the rest of us accord ourselves. The task is to change her former rule which tells her she must not ever make a mistake into one which says mistakes are what people learn from, so go ahead – make a mistake, learn from it and then go ahead and make another different mistake and learn from that. Just don't go on making the same (anorexic?) mistake over and over again.

The question of where and with whom to live is almost certain to arise even if the anorexic has been in her parents' home throughout the illness or established elsewhere for the whole time. A change was probably likely even had she not been ill. In this, as with the choice of job, she may soon wish to reverse her first decision. Experience often shatters cherished illusions and the dream of independent living can be a disappointment in reality. Sometimes a new relationship whose establishment seems to proclaim total emancipation from dependence on parents turns out to be merely a transfer of that dependence to someone else, husband, lover or flatmates. She will learn, as so many of us have learnt, that it need not always be a disaster to get things wrong the first time.

In the process of surviving these ups and downs of post-anorexic life the recovering anorexic, increasingly in touch with her own spontaneous feelings and learning to trust them, becomes able to accept not only her own shortcomings but also the imperfections of others. She stops seeing it as all right or totally wrong and begins, in Matthew Arnold's words, to 'see life steadily and see it whole.'

The fact that so many severely anorexic sufferers have survived the experience triumphantly makes it all the more distressing to recognise that there are still a number (perhaps one

The Eating Sickness

in five) in whom the symptoms of the illness have become a chronic feature of their lives. Whatever help they may have had has proved ineffective; they may have had none or they may have been unable to complete the arduous recovery course through which others have struggled to success. They may, in fact, never have embarked on it if no one has been able to instil in them enough confidence and sense of their own worth and value to inspire the effort. In Chapter 5 this kindling of motivation in the anorexic patient was defined as an essential for the initiation of therapy. What does not begin cannot finish and, however long and hard everyone concerned may strive to 'cure' an anorexic sufferer, no real progress will take place until she herself becomes actively engaged in the process.

The simple answer to the question of who gets better from anorexia nervosa might be, therefore, those who want, or who can be inspired to want, to do all the hard work that is needed, and those who find and can use the kind of help most effective for them. And our definition 'better' would mean not exactly as before but *better* than before with increased confidence and greater enjoyment of life despite whatever regrets may still linger until they are finally dispersed by happiness and the passage of time. No longer is time experienced as a dreadful void which has to be filled with unrelenting dutiful activity. Instead it often goes too fast and is crowded with a variety of experiences which each day can bring some moment of spontaneous delight, whether through learning or sense experience or new friendship. At last it is possible to have fun, to receive and just to be.

No one in the grip of anorexia nervosa's harsh demands can ever stop to consider the lilies, how they grow. She would disapprove of the fact that they toil not, neither do they spin – but once recovered she cannot merely see them and stop to admire their beauty but also at appropriate times and seasons revel in following their example.

10 Hail and Farewell

When considering whether or not to read a particular book many people (ourselves included) habitually turn to the final pages hoping that a concluding summary will help with the decision. This chapter, therefore, is dedicated as much to the interests of prospective readers as to those of other readers who may have worked their way to this point from the beginning of the volume. It is intended to clarify for those about to set out, where they are going and for those who have already come this far, where they have been.

We have tried throughout this book to adhere to two guiding principles.

The first principle was that nothing should be included which had not, in some way, formed part of our own experience of living and working for nine years in close daily contact with the phenomena of eating disorders. One inevitable result of basing our observations and commentary on what has become increasingly familiar to us is a degree of subjectivity which may be regarded as inimical to a strictly scientific approach. In Chapter 1 however we have explained our belief that a totally objective approach to an illness which is a manifestation of a subjective experience is unlikely to lead to a lasting cure. In subsequent chapters we have attempted to substantiate this claim, and to show that how things are done (and experienced) is actually far more important than what is done.

Our second aim was the extension of the field of vision beyond the focal point of the sufferers themselves to include the background or setting in which their difficulties occurred. In doing this we have tried to accord due importance to a considered understanding of the experiences and feelings of the relatives, friends and therapists of those who succumb to an eating sickness.

These two aims represent, roughly, the twin aspects of our dual authorship; the designated patient being primarily the concern of the doctor while her co-author concerns herself with the rest. This bipartite arrangement reflects the manner in which a doctor or medical therapist and co-worker may on occasion be partners in the treatment of those patients for whom such a pattern of care is appropriate. In such a partnership the two areas of interest are not mutually exclusive and the endeavours of each are complementary rather than supplementary to those of the other.

The way in which such a partnership may assist the process of recovery from anorexia nervosa has been described in Chapter 8 but it is hoped that our ideas about this, as about other pertinent matters, can be seen as part of the pervading theme of the book.

Although it was conceived as a unitary whole the division into chapters aims at clarifying rather than complicating the issues which so often bewilder those who seek to understand the illness and for whom this book was written.

It was also written to be read in sequence but, since we recognise this as a hope rather than an expectation, an additional aim has been to give each chapter its own separate coherence. This results in some inevitable repetition of, or reference to, observations made in previous chapters and in a different context.

Finally it was written for anyone who, for whatever reason, wonders whether they might find within it something which can help them, or someone dear to them. The hope that they will do so, whoever they may be, is the theme and purpose of this book.

Index